JOHN BROWN

UNIVERSITY OF VIRGINIA PRESS

CHARLOTTESVILLE AND LONDON

··· The Legend Revisited

JOHN BROWN

MERRILL D. PETERSON

University of Virginia Press
© 2002 by the Rector and Visitors of the University of Virginia
All rights reserved
Printed in the United States of America on acid-free paper
First published 2002

9 8 7 6 5 4 3 2 1

TITLE PAGE ART: A detail from *The Tragic Prelude,* mural by John Steuart Curry, Kansas Statehouse, Topeka. (Courtesy of the Kansas State Historical Society)

LIBRARY OF CONGRESS CATALOGING-IN-PUBLICATION DATA
Peterson, Merrill D.
    John Brown : the legend revisited / Merrill D. Peterson.
        p.   cm.
Includes bibliographical references and index.
        ISBN 0-8139-2132-5 (alk. paper)
        1. Brown, John 1800–1859.   2. Abolitionists—United States—Biography.
    3. Antislavery movements—United States—History—19th century.   I. Title.
    E451.B8786 P47 2002
    973.7′116′092—dc21   2002005173

TO

Jeff, Ida, and Jamie
Kent and Janet
& Nini

Contents

Illustrations

Acknowledgments

For research on this book I am once again indebted to the Alderman Library of the University of Virginia, above all to Doug Hurd and Lou Purifoy of the Interlibrary Loan Division. The Virginia Historical Society and the Library of Virginia made useful contributions. At that national treasure, the Library of Congress, I owe special thanks to Pamella Russell for her guidance through the labyrinth of divisions; and particularly to Jeff Flannery and company in Manuscripts and Maja Keech and Mary Isonin in Prints and Photographs. Baker Library of Columbia University spread before me the John Brown Collection assembled by Oswald Garrison Villard. The Ohio Historical Society and the Kansas State Historical Society made valuable contributions. A hurried visit to the Oberlin College Library proved worth the effort. And I cannot say enough in praise of the John Brown Collection of the Hudson, Ohio, Library and Museum, or of the hospitality and guidance of Thomas L. Vince, who helped establish it, and of James F. Coccamo, its curator. Historical sites, monuments, and museums have left vivid impressions. While writing a book of this sort, fugitive aid comes from unexpected sources; in this instance allow me to thank Thomas Klein of Chicago, Bill Theriault of Bakerton, West Virginia, and Mr. and Mrs. Fontaine B. Hoof of Wheeling, West Virginia. Luckily, I drew a superb copyeditor, Barbara H. Salazar of Ithaca, New York, and I have expressed my appreciation to her.

The pleasure of the research and writing would have been incalculably less but for the constant presence and the contributions of my dear friend Nini Almy.

In the way of permissions I owe thanks to Michael S. Harper and the University of Illinois Press to quote from *Images of Kin: New and Selected Poems* (1977) and to Maia Patillo for selected quotation of the poem on John Brown in Robert Hayden's *Collected Poems* (1985).

This book is an extended meditation on the life of John Brown and his place in American thought and imagination from the time of his death in 1859 to the near-present. To that extent it bears a certain relationship to two of my earlier works: *The Jefferson Image in the American Mind* (1960) and *Lincoln in American Memory* (1994). The book would not have been written at all but for a casual reading of Russell Banks's historical novel *Cloudsplitter*, which opened to me a view of John Brown I had not had before and spurred me to learn more about his life and legend.

JOHN BROWN

The John Brown Epoch

NEWS OF the raid on the federal arsenal at Harpers Ferry, Virginia, sped like lightning over the telegraph wires Monday morning, October 17, 1859. The conductor of the train bound eastward for Baltimore sounded the alarm. "They say they have come to free the slaves and intend to do it at all hazards." That was enough to cause the head of the Baltimore and Ohio Railroad to alert the president of the United States, James Buchanan, and Governor Henry A. Wise of Virginia. The first newspaper reports were exaggerated and confused. No sooner was the leader of the invasion identified as Osawatomie John Brown, well known for his exploits in "Bleeding Kansas," than he and his small force — sixteen whites and five blacks — were killed, run off, or captured. They had been overpowered by local militia, reinforced by a company of U.S. Marines under the command of Colonel Robert E. Lee. The next day Captain Brown bowed to Lee's surrender terms. Two of his sons had already been killed, and Old Brown himself was wounded in the course of surrender.

Governor Wise, a wily political veteran, hurried to Harpers Ferry to take charge of rapidly unfolding events there. Situated at the mountainous juncture of the Shenandoah and Potomac rivers, famously described by Thomas Jefferson, Harpers Ferry lay within U.S. jurisdiction, and the attack upon it might have been made the nation's business; but President Buchanan acquiesced in the governor's preemptory move. Wise's political enemies saw it as a typically demagogic stroke in his pursuit of the Democratic presidential nomination a year hence. Wise, with others, interviewed Brown in the crowded paymaster's office, where he lay on the floor wounded, his clothes, face, hair, hands smeared with blood. The anger the governor felt toward the captive was filtered through layers of feelings of disgrace and dishonor inflicted on the proud commonwealth by a pitiful force of lightly armed men. Brown talked freely and cheerfully. When the governor suggested he should set his mind on eternity, Brown answered smartly, "You are not likely to be more than fifteen or twenty years behind me in the journey to eternity, a very trifling distance, and I want *you* to be prepared; whether I go in fifteen months or fifteen hours, I am prepared to go; you Slaveholders have a heavy responsibility, and it behooves you to prepare more than it does me."[1] He steadfastly refused to implicate others, taking full responsibility for the raid and its failure upon himself. On October 20, in nearby Charles Town, seat of Jefferson County, where the prisoners had been removed, Governor Wise appeared before a magistrate charging Brown and his fellow captives with murder and diverse crimes.

After his return to Richmond, the governor made a public address upon the events at Harpers Ferry. On the one hand, he congratulated the people on the failure of the raid to incite a single slave to break his bonds; on the other hand, voicing fears for the safety of the commonwealth, he implored the citizens to organize and arm in self-defense. Of John Brown himself he spoke with more than a trace of admiration. "They are mistaken who take him to be a madman. He is a bundle of the best nerves I ever saw—cut and thrust and bleeding in bonds. He is a man of clear head, of courage, of simple ingenuousness. He is cool, collected, and indomitable."[2] Crack the molds and change the occasion, a northerner would observe, and these two, the governor and the prisoner, would be friends rather than enemies.

·· How came John Brown to Harpers Ferry in his fifty-ninth year? Descended from the earliest colonists of New England, he was born in Torrington, Connecticut, into a respectable family of ordinary means. Both his father and grandfather had served in the Revolutionary War. When he was five, he moved with his family to Ohio, and thus overlaid the deep strain of Calvinist piety in his nature with the ruggedness of frontier ways. He followed his father, Owen, into the tanning trade, but as was customary in a new country, Brown turned his hand to many things. He was a shepherd, a farmer, a surveyor, and a wool merchant. Schooling was "fitful and scanty," as a biographer has said. Brown, however, read a small shelf of literary classics from Plutarch to Benjamin Franklin; he admired the character and achievements of military heroes, especially Oliver Cromwell and Napoleon; and, of course, he knew the Bible by heart. Twice married, Brown fathered twenty children, of whom thirteen lived to maturity. A rigid disciplinarian, he was also a tender and devoted father. The family lived for a time in Pennsylvania, but returned to Ohio's Western Reserve in 1835. Soon Brown discovered his divine mission: to free the country of slavery. (Asked by an interlocutor after his capture at Harpers Ferry, "Do you consider yourself an instrument in the hands of Providence?" Brown answered without hesitation, "I do.")[3] Brown's empathy with blacks was the most remarkable feature of his character. He truly believed that black people were the equals of whites, and he conducted himself accordingly.

In 1846, as the country went to war with Mexico, Brown resettled in Springfield, Massachusetts, the better to carry on the wool business of the Ohio partnership of Perkins & Brown. Here he formed closer connection with abolitionists, though he dissented from the platform of the Massachusetts Anti-Slavery Society, under the sway of William Lloyd Garrison. He could not accept the sufficiency of moral suasion to end slavery, nor could he agree with the doctrine of "no Union with slaveholders." Brown launched his own militant League of Gileadites to prepare the black people to defend themselves and fight for their freedom. To Brown's simple home on Franklin Street, Frederick Douglass, the notable black freedman and abolitionist, who also opposed Garrisonism, came to visit him. Douglass shared a hearty meal with the patriarch and his family and learned of Brown's secret plan to organize a force of liberated slaves in the Appalachian Mountains to strike for their freedom. Douglass was impressed. In his autobiography he left this description of the man: "In person he was lean, strong, and sinewy, of the best New England mold. . . . Clad in plain American woolen, shod in boots of cowhide leather, and wearing a cravat . . . , under six feet high, less than 150 pounds in weight, and aged about fifty, he preserved a figure straight and symmetrical as a mountain pine." He went on to speak of Brown's elongated head, graying hair, clean-shaven face, prominent chin, and popping blue-gray eyes. "When on the street, he moved with a long, springing, race-horse step, absorbed by his own reflections."[4]

Brown's business ventures, including Perkins & Brown, always ended in failure. In 1848, anxious to proceed with the Lord's business, Brown entered into a plan developed by the wealthy New York landholder-philanthropist Gerrit Smith to settle black colonists on a 120,000-acre tract in the Adirondack wilderness. With Smith's help he acquired a small farm in a place called North Elba, where he hoped not only to support his own family but also to put his farming skills to the use of the black colonists. A further consideration was that Westport, on Lake Champlain, not far distant, was a station on the Underground Railroad. Wherever he lived, John Brown aided in the work of guiding fugitive slaves to freedom under the North Star. To his humble abode came a tramping itinerant from Boston, the author Richard Henry Dana Jr., who left a record of the visit in his diary. Despite the primitive appearance of the cabin overshadowed by forest, its principal occupant, "a man named Brown," was well informed on most subjects, had books, and boasted the best cattle around. The meal was in neighborly style. "Mr. and Mrs. Brown and their large family of children with the hired men and women, including the negroes, all at the table together." It was neat, substantial, and wholesome, said Dana; and all in the household, including the blacks, were called by surnames with the prefix "Mr." or "Mrs." "How mysterious," he would later write of this encounter, "is the touch of fate which gives man immortality on earth!"[5] The Adirondack experiment was a pipe dream, as Brown must soon have realized, yet the North Elba farm was the nearest thing to home he ever had.

In August 1855 John Brown followed six of his sons to Kansas, newly opened to settlement by the Kansas-Nebraska Act. The sons went mainly with a view to staking a claim and making a life on the fertile prairie; their father went to save the land from the harlot slavery. The act organizing the territory repealed the Missouri Compromise, which had closed this land to slavery, and referred the decision on that question to the will of the people ("popular sovereignty") when they framed a constitution and applied for statehood. As a result, Kansas at once became a battleground between pro- and anti-slavery forces. In this contest the former held the advantage initially because Kansas bordered on Missouri, a slave state, and because the administration in Washington under President Franklin Pierce openly sided with the South. In the North the new opposition Republican Party was committed to "free soil," and the New England Emigrant Aid Company took the lead in furnishing colonists as well as arms for Kansas.

Arriving at Osawatomie, near the primitive family settlement in eastern Kansas, Brown soon made his presence known to the Free State leadership at Lawrence and was named captain of a company of "Liberty Guards." After a brief truce between the hostile camps, one dedicated to freedom, the other to slavery, each with its own government, Bleeding Kansas began to bleed in earnest. The "Border Ruffians" sacked and burned Lawrence. Brown, with his party, was rushing to the town's defense when he learned it had been destroyed, so he turned back, and at a place on Pottawatomie Creek presided over the murder of five slave-state settlers. The precise circumstances and motives were wrapped in obscurity when Brown went on trial in Virginia three years later; but the Pottawatomie Massacre was destined to become the blackest blot on John Brown's escutcheon. About this time the Kansas fever invaded the United States Senate when a South Carolina congressman beat senseless Charles Sumner, of Massachusetts, in retaliation for his speech "The Crime against Kansas."

Brown became the terror of the prairie in 1856. Reporters for eastern newspapers lionized him. His fame increased in June with the defeat of a superior force under the Border Ruffian captain Henry Clay Pate at a place called Black Jack. It was sealed at Osawatomie in the fall. Here a cavalry force of 250, mounted and armed in Missouri under command of veteran officers of the Mexican War, undertook to wipe out Brown, his family, and his allies. Outnumbered 10 to 1, they fought gamely but went down in defeat. Brown's son Frederick lost his life; the captain himself was reported killed; the town was consumed in flames. "God sees it," Brown said as he watched, then, face wet with tears, vowed to his son Jason, "I have only a short time to live—only one death to die, and I will die fighting for this cause. There will be no peace in this land until slavery is done for. I will give them something else to do than to extend slave territory. I will carry the war into Africa."[6] Henceforth he was known as "Old Osawatomie Brown."

In the fall, during a lull in the fighting, Brown returned to the East. After a brief reunion with his North Elba family, he traveled to Boston with the aim of arousing support for the Kansas cause. A call on Franklin B. Sanborn, the young secretary of the Massachusetts Kansas Committee, won Brown not only a valued ally but a worshipful advocate through a long life. Sanborn introduced Brown to a coterie of influential friends, abolitionists all: Theodore Parker, the famous Boston preacher and reformer; Samuel Gridley Howe, humanitarian and philanthropist; George Luther Stearns, a well-to-do industrialist; and Thomas Wentworth Higginson, Worcester pastor and author. Together with Brown's friend Gerrit Smith, of Peter-boro, New York, they composed the Secret Six, as they would come to be known for their aid and counsel to Brown. Sanborn, a Concord schoolmaster, also introduced the old warrior to his literary elders Ralph Waldo Emerson and Henry David Thoreau, and arranged for him to address the Massachusetts legislature, which then had under consideration an appropriation in aid of freedom in Kansas. Brown spoke movingly of his experiences. The address raised his fame but failed to secure the public aid he had hoped for. After a visit to New York, where he made new friends but got disappointingly little in the way of aid, he set out for Kansas with Sharps rifles, sundry supplies, and hard cash to an estimated value of some $13,000.

The prospects for peace and freedom in Kansas had brightened. Brown turned his attention primarily to the project he had been turning over in his head for twenty years: to scurry up bands of fugitive blacks in the southern mountains to fight for their freedom and undermine the institution of slavery in every way they could. He steadily lost confidence in abolitionists who were unprepared to act. "These men are all talk. What is needed is action—action!"[7] He began at this time to grow the beard that would become his most distinguishing feature. In the East he had met a military adventurer, Hugh Forbes, who had fought with Giuseppe Garibaldi in Italy and was attracted to Brown's enterprise. He was employed to train the recruits gathered in Tabor, Iowa, near the Missouri and Nebraska borders, in guerrilla tactics. In May 1858 Brown and his confederates assembled in convention at Chatham, Canada West, across the border from Detroit. Here they adopted a provisional constitution drafted by their leader for the conduct of government in liberated territory. At this time Brown expected to launch the invasion in the fall; and after the convention Brown hastened to Boston to secure further backing from his friends. A disappointed Forbes, however, believing he had been misled, threatened to betray the secret. This development upset everything. The captain was reluctant to postpone the invasion, but the Secret Six persuaded him to do so.

John Brown, daguerreotype by Augustus Washington, 1847

National Portrait Gallery, Smithsonian Institution; purchased with major acquisition
funds and with funds donated by Betty Adler Schermer in honor of her great-grandfather
August M. Bondi

So Brown once more returned to Kansas, this time with an alias,
Shubel Morgan, and a flowing beard. His principal exploit, in December, was a raid across the Missouri border to liberate eleven
slaves. It was executed with finesse, barring the unfortunate death of
an innocent Missourian. In addition to the slaves, Brown and his

men made off with horses, wagons, and provisions. Outraged editorials appeared in Missouri newspapers. The governor, it was reported, offered a $3,000 reward for the capture of the outlaw Brown; and his arrest was also ordered by President Buchanan, who added $250 to the price on his head. The raid was not designed as a test for Brown's operations in the Appalachians, yet it had that character. Taking charge of the freed blacks, John Brown personally led them some 1,500 miles in the dead of winter along the western Underground Railroad, through Iowa, thence to Chicago and Detroit, finally to Windsor in Canada.

In March 1859 Brown was lecturing in Cleveland. The city editor of the *Plain Dealer,* the humorist Artemus Ward, wrote a memorable description of him:

> He is a medium-sized, compactly built and wiry man, and as quick as a cat in his movements. His hair is of salt and pepper hue and as stiff as bristles, he has a long, waving milk-white goatee, which gives him a somewhat patriarchal appearance, his eyes are gray and sharp. A man of pluck is Brown. . . . Turn him into a ring with nine Border Ruffians, four bears, and six Injuns and a brace of bull pups, and we opine that "the eagles of victory would perch on his banner."[8]

Brown apologized for the Missouri horses he had "liberated," saying, "They are Abolition horses. . . . I converted them." As for the president's bounty of $250 for his head, Brown responded with a $2.50 reward for Buchanan's. He went on to Peterboro, to North Elba, thence to Concord and Boston. He took counsel with the Secret Six. They continued to support his invasion plan, though none understood it in detail. In July he rented Kennedy Farm in Maryland, five or six miles from Harpers Ferry. The farm was the staging area for the raid. In August he had a secret meeting with Frederick Douglass in nearby Chambersburg, Pennsylvania. He had counted on Douglass to join him. But the black leader, to whom he disclosed his plan more fully than to anyone else, thought it suicidal and declined. His

John Brown, photograph attributed to James Wallace Black, 1859
National Portrait Gallery, Smithsonian Institution

young black companion, Shields Green, however, decided to go with the old man. He eventually met his death on the gallows.

•• A T F I R S T the American people responded to the raid at Harpers Ferry with varying degrees of dismay and disapproval. Nobody had a good word to say about it. It was a terrible failure, of course, and whether viewed as tragedy or as farce, it was dismissed as the act of a madman. "Monomania" was the term commonly given to Brown's delirium. Some traced it to the sufferings he had endured in Kansas or, more particularly, to fury over the violent death of his son Frederick. A Richmond newspaper called the invasion "a miserably weak and contemptible affair," while the *National Era,* the abolitionist weekly in Washington, opined, "The cause of emancipation had no worse enemies than these men."[9] The editor had in mind the potentially damaging effect of the affair on the Republican Party in the North. Brown's brush would be used to tar every Republican leader beginning with William H. Seward, the New York senator and presidential aspirant, who had described the sectional struggle as an "irrepressible conflict." The recovery of a trunk full of papers the captain had carelessly left behind at Kennedy Farm implicated such prominent antislavery leaders as Joshua R. Giddings and Gerrit Smith in Brown's project and also turned up crude maps and related documents suggesting that he intended to move deeper into the southern Appalachians. Hugh Forbes's revelations gave credence to the ideas of conspiracy involving prominent antislavery Republicans. No evidence of partisan affiliation or purpose on Brown's part ever surfaced, but this did not prevent major Democratic newspapers— the *Herald* in New York, the *Post* in Boston—from harping on the connection. A week after the raid Giddings published his denial of prior knowledge or complicity in Brown's enterprise. Members of the Secret Six, who had more than a passing acquaintance with it, kept silent. Two of them, Stearns and Howe, decamped to Canada; a third, Smith, lapsed into insanity. Douglass, though not one of the group, sailed for England.

In the South contempt quickly gave way to fear. Trifling though Brown's sting was, the *Charleston Mercury* editorialized, it was "a portentous omen of the future." It proved for one last time that there was no peace for the South in the Union. The newspaper ran an account of a discourse, "The Weakness and Final Doom of Slavery," by the Reverend Henry Highland Garnet, preached to his black congregation in New York the Sunday after the raid.[10] The sermon was laced with prophetic scriptural passages. People asked what good the raid did. Garnet answered: It made slaveholders think that if this big a disturbance could be set off by a handful of men, what might be done with more? There was nothing left for the South but to arm, said the *Mercury*. The newly inaugurated governor of the Palmetto State, William H. Gist, took up the call in his message to the legislature. Newspapers around the state and in neighboring states ascribed every petty crime—barn burning, for instance—to agents of John Brown, and vigilantes went into action. Militant southern disunionists already had on their agenda a plan to reopen the slave trade. The raid set that plan back. It came as well at a time when the whole South was reeling under the blows delivered by Hinton R. Helper's *Impending Crisis,* a book that documented the South's economic and cultural backwardness in comparison with the North. A correspondent expressed his frustration in the *Mercury:* "The merchant princes and cotton lords of the North fatten on our products, and with this wealth send us, in return, the wolves and tigers of Harper's Ferry."[11] The only consolation the Charleston editor could take from the event was that it had brought Virginia back into the fold of the South after pursuing a wavering sort of neutrality for many years.

As it happened, the regular session of the Jefferson County Circuit Court, in Charles Town, Virginia, began on October 20, and so John Brown's trial was docketed for the 25th. This unseemly haste, taken to dispel panic, was the first of several issues of fairness raised by the trial. The criminally accused, still suffering from his wounds and lying on a cot before the bar, was hardly in condition to defend himself. Moreover, he had had no opportunity to obtain counsel, and very soon repudiated the counsel assigned for his defense. He was accused of treason, murder, and incitement of slave insurrection. The idea of treason as a crime against a state, Virginia, especially by one not a citizen, was a novelty, and under other circumstances might have been contested. So, too, might the selection of an impartial jury in a court verging on the scene of crimes as notorious as those alleged. Brown, however, although he dismissed the trial as a farce, resigned himself to his fate. The only one of the three charges he disputed was that of inciting insurrection among the slaves. He came to free the slaves, of course, but not to incite rebellion or to carry them off; his purpose, he protested, was to put them in a position to defend themselves.

Before a fair-minded judge, Richard Parker, the trial proceeded without interruption during six days in the packed chamber of the dignified but dingy courthouse. Only approved reporters were allowed in the chamber. Governor Wise's handpicked prosecutor, Andrew Hunter, told the jurors that the attack on Harpers Ferry was part of a larger conspiracy to embroil the nation in war over slavery. Hunter had not gone far before Brown's counsel, John Minor Botts, soon to be dismissed, said he had received information of insanity in Brown's family and pleaded for delay to investigate this line of defense. Brown was indignant. While acknowledging some evidence of instability on his mother's side of the family, he could not tolerate any defamation of his motive against slavery. (Emerson, in faraway Concord, noted in his journal that what lawyers call insanity is precisely "being governed by an ideal.") In due course, more trustworthy counsel arrived from the North to conduct Brown's defense. In truth, however, there was no defense. Or confession, or apology, or extenuation, only a plea of faithfulness to a divinely ordained mission.

Brown was convicted on all counts. Counsel moved for arrest of judgment for errors in both the indictment and the verdict. On December 2 Judge Parker ruled against the motion, then before passing sentence asked the defendant if he had anything to say. Taken by surprise, Brown rose, according to a *New-York Tribune* reporter, and with his hands on the table before him spoke haltingly in a gentle voice. "The types can give you no intimation of the soft and tender tones, yet calm and manly, withal, that filled the court-room, and, I think," wrote the reporter, "touched the hearts of many who had come only to rejoice at the heaviest blow their victim was to suffer."[12]

This man at the bar was, for all his fame, so little known in the North and the South that his speech to the court, entirely impromptu, attracted much interest and in many eyes sealed his fame as hero and martyr. He began by denying everything except what he had all along admitted: a design to free slaves. He had hoped "to make a clean thing of the matter," as he had done in Missouri, "without the snapping of a gun on either side." "I never intended murder or treason or the destruction of property or to excite or incite Slaves to rebellion or to make an insurrection." He then made an analogy that placed his crime in a larger context. "Had I so interfered in behalf of the rich, the powerful, the intelligent, the so called great . . . and suffered and sacrificed what I have in this interference, it would have been all right, and every man in this court would have deemed it an act worthy of reward rather than punishment." He pleaded the justice of his motives and purposes in the eyes of God. The court apparently acknowledged it.

> I see the book kissed, which I suppose to be the Bible . . . which teaches me that all things whatsoever I would that men should do to me, I should do even so to them. It teaches me further to remember them that are in bonds as bound with them. I endeavor to act up to that instruction. . . . Now, if it is deemed necessary that I should forfeit my life for the furtherance of the ends of justice, and mingle my blood further with the blood of my children and with the blood of millions of this Slave-country, whose rights are disregarded by wicked, cruel, and unjust enactments, I say let it be done.[13]

Brown went on to discourage legal efforts in his behalf by expressing himself satisfied with his trial. Whatever procedural errors there may have been, he seemed to say he had received substantial justice. At the same time, he felt no consciousness of guilt. He concluded with a blanket dismissal of statements bruited about that some of his confederates had been wrongly induced and misled to join him. On the contrary, all had come of their own accord and largely at their own expense. "Now I have done." The judge then pronounced sentence of death by hanging one month hence. But for one pair of clapped hands, it was heard with profound silence in the courtroom.[14] Trial of Brown's fellow prisoners had already begun.

• • THE SENTENCE seemed to say that "While Brown lives, Virginia is in peril," Horace Greeley's *Tribune* observed. A second invasion scare came in the middle of November. Fears of attempts to rescue the prisoners compounded the panic aroused by unrest among the slaves. An unprecedented number of fires were reported in the county. Governor Wise ordered more troops to Charles Town. Pennsylvania's governor reportedly tendered 10,000 militiamen to aid Virginia—an offer Wise indignantly refused. The fears were a reminder of the South's vulnerability, and the execution of John Brown was unlikely to allay them. The governor might commute his sentence or even pardon him, citing evidence of insanity. This was the advice given to him by the most influential pro-slavery newspaper in the North, the *New York Journal of Commerce*. Unhappily, the governor had drawn a very large elephant at Harpers Ferry, and it wasn't at all clear what to do with him. "To hang a fanatic is to make a martyr of him and fledge another brood of the same sort," said the *Journal*. "Better send these creatures to the penitentiary, and so make of them miserable felons."[15] This might have been good advice, but the people of Virginia would never condone it, nor could the governor admit he had been victimized by a crazy man. The *Richmond Enquirer,* edited by Wise's son, chaffed about trading the lives of Brown and his men for the lives of those who had made him a fanatic:

"Bring Seward, Greeley, Giddings, [John P.] Hale, and Smith to the jurisdiction of Virginia, and Brown and his deluded victims in Charles Town jail may hope for pardon." [16]

All the while waves of sympathy rolled over John Brown in the North. Set in motion by his noble conduct during the trial, above all by his speech to the court, the current of sympathy was influenced as well by letters from prison passed to the press and by noteworthy speeches made in his behalf. The redoubtable Henry Ward Beecher, while no supporter of Brown, preached a sermon at Brooklyn's Plymouth Church the Sunday before his sentencing that caught up in a few words the power he had come to embody. "Let no man pray that Brown be spared," Beecher said. "Let Virginia make him a martyr. Now he has only blundered. His soul was noble; his work miserable. But a cord and a gibbet would redeem all that, and round up Brown's failure with a heroic success." The prisoner, upon reading these words in his cell, wrote in the margin, "good." [17]

Wendell Phillips, for a quarter-century the mighty orator of the abolitionist movement, spoke often and well during the John Brown epoch. At Beecher's church on the Tuesday after the sermon, Phillips declared that "the lesson of the hour is insurrection." That was, in fact, always Phillips's message; but in Brown he found a man—"a regular Cromwellian dug up from two centuries"—ready to die for an idea rather than simply agitate for it. [18] Henry Thoreau, the New England Transcendentalist, had been transfixed by Captain Brown when he earlier heard him speak in Concord. On October 30, while Brown was still on trial, Thoreau lectured on him as if he were already a sainted martyr. He described him as a rough-hewn Yankee who went to school in the West and "a transcendentalist above all, a man of ideas and principles." To those who say he threw his life away, Thoreau asked "which way they threw their lives, pray?" No American had ever stood more heroically for the idea upon which the country was founded. "It was his peculiar doctrine that a man has a perfect right to interfere by force with the slaveholder, in order to rescue the slave. I agree with him." This sentiment, coming from a man who some years before wrote a celebrated essay advocating passive resistance, surprised many people. But Thoreau's defense of John Brown's force was only the other face of the doctrine that proclaimed, basically, the superiority of conscience over the state and its laws. By teaching Americans how to live, the hero of Harpers Ferry might finally teach them how to die. That was his best legacy. "Perhaps he saw it himself. I *almost fear,*" said Thoreau, "that I may yet hear of his deliverance, doubting if a prolonged life, if *any* life, can do as much good as his death."[19]

Such words and feelings helped to change the mind of the North about John Brown. Lunatic! Fanatic! Incompetent! Traitor! The language of disparagement and dishonor that had rained upon Brown immediately after the ill-starred invasion gave way to a chorus of respect, admiration, and praise. The editors of the *Boston Daily Advertiser,* addressing the change of sentiment, said, "His act may stand as a symbolical expression of the intense hatred of slavery entertained by a man of integrity and courage, and so may work out good in the ultimate dispensation of Providence." The *Chicago Tribune,* which had called Brown insane, now said he had done the antislavery cause yeoman service and taught the country the costs of human freedom; the weekly Congregational magazine, the *Independent,* said that the moral dignity of the perpetrator redeemed the crime; while the *National Era,* in a thoughtful editorial, "The Sober Second Thought," sought to make Harpers Ferry a wake-up call to the slaveholding South. Six weeks earlier the blessings of the system had been a daily theme of eulogy; now it excited fear and dread. Taking a leaf from the past, the editor invoked the precedent of the bloody Nat Turner insurrection, in 1831, which had led to the critical and the last Virginia slavery debate, believing that though it failed, another hard look might yet succeed in abolishing the system.[20] John Brown's murderous raid recalled to Americans Thomas Jefferson's jeremiad against slavery: "And can the liberties of a nation be thought secure when we have removed their only firm basis, a conviction in the minds of the people that these liberties are the gift of God? That they are not to be violated but with his wrath? Indeed I tremble for my country when I reflect that God is just: that his justice cannot sleep forever."[21]

Virginia, with the South, however, drew a different lesson from Harpers Ferry. A *Tribune* reporter, in a dispatch from Petersburg, wrote of the bitterness and rancor against the North that had taken possession of the community. He quoted a leading lawyer: "I would be glad to see the whole North sink to the deepest depth of the bottomless pit! Damn her!" Southern newspapers picked up the change of opinion about John Brown in the northern press, platform, and pulpit. "The entire press of the North unites in begging off the criminal," said the *Richmond Dispatch*. Repeatedly its editor denounced "the Puritan Press of the North" and accused great ministers, such as Beecher, of converting the pulpit into a secular political engine. Why had this happened? Fundamentally, said the editor, because of the opposite cultural lineages of North and South, one Puritan, the other Cavalier. John Brown exemplified the Cromwellian stock, somber, stark, and secretive. And it quoted Brown himself, who in rejecting visits by Virginia ministers of the Gospel said, "We do not worship the same God." All this resonated with sounds of disunion. In New Orleans, *De Bow's Review,* the journal of southern industry and progress, saw in the Harpers Ferry raid "the first act in the grand tragedy of emancipation . . . the vanguard of the great army intended for our subjugation."[22]

In their personal letters, thoughtful Virginians could not disguise their sense of betrayal over the outrage. Thus Nathaniel Cabell, a leading citizen of Nelson County, tried to convey his feelings to the prominent New Yorker and Jefferson biographer Henry S. Randall. Referring less to the event, which to him was a trifle, than to the sequel, Cabell said, "It was as if an intrusive reptile should strike at the heel of a man who, suspecting nothing, was walking peacefully in his own garden," only then to realize that the reptile had been sent by a professed friend and brother. Southerners had thought, Cabell continued, that "conservative, right-thinking men at the North" understood them. But no. "They have remained, in a degree, passive, while the immense tide of calumny against the Institutions and People of the South have been flowing apace." So the South must think of declaring its independence, becoming Spartans, and taking John C. Calhoun rather than Jefferson as its patron saint and guide.[23]

Perhaps the most interesting literary product of the John Brown epoch was the pamphlet *Correspondence between Lydia Maria Child and Gov. Wise and Mrs. Mason of Virginia.* It did not appear in this form until 1860, when it sold 300,000 copies; but portions of the correspondence turned up in the press during John Brown's imprisonment. Mrs. Child, of Massachusetts, was a novelist and biographer as well as a veteran abolitionist author. When Brown came to trial she wrote disarmingly to Governor Wise: "I have heard that you were a man of chivalrous sentiments." So she asked the governor to read and transmit her letter to the prisoner and also for permission to visit and comfort him. Along with everyone else, she had been incredulous about the raid, yet with her friends felt "a natural impulse of sympathy for a brave and suffering man." In her letter to Brown, Mrs. Child, as a believer in "peace principles," disavowed his methods, yet was moved by his sacrifice on behalf of the blacks. "In brief, I love you and bless you." Governor Wise, in reply, said he had a constitutional obligation to allow visits to the prisoner, but he strongly advised her against it. Mrs. Child expressed wonder over the governor's constitutional scruples. Where slavery was concerned, they were commonly held in disregard south of the Potomac. She cited the notorious case of Samuel Hoar, who, on a lawful mission on behalf of Massachusetts colored seamen wrongly imprisoned in South Carolina, was publicly humiliated and turned back. She cited the case of a bookseller forced to flee for his life in Mobile, and the case of a professor expelled for teaching against slavery at the University of North Carolina. As for Brown, he was no criminal but a martyr to right and liberty. She accused the governor of "premeditated treason," since he had threatened secession if a Republican were elected president in 1860. Mrs. Child scored her best hit by reference to the

Great Seal of Virginia on the governor's letterhead: a liberty-loving heroine with her foot on a prostrate despot, bearing the legend "Sic Semper Tyrannus." A remarkable sentiment for the slaveholding governor!

The prisoner, too, discouraged Mrs. Child's visit; and so she gave it up. Meanwhile, Governor Wise, having passed this exchange of letters to the press, also sent it to the wife of James M. Mason, Virginia's senior senator. She undertook to lecture Mrs. Child on tendering her sympathy to suffering subjects nearer at hand, such as the "wage slaves" in northern factories. "Do you read your Bible, Mrs. Child?" she asked, then cited chapter and verse condoning slavery. Mrs. Child fired back chapter and verse of her own selection. As the correspondence drew to a close, the author came to believe, with other peace-principled abolitionists, that there could be no peace for slaveholders after John Brown's moral example. "To all outward appearances," Mrs. Child wrote privately, "all is defeat and ruin. Yet in reality what a glorious success! What a splendid martyrdom. The scaffold will be as glorious as the Cross of Calvary."[24]

Mary Day Brown, having made the arduous journey from North Elba to Charles Town, met and talked with her husband the day before his execution. When she passed through Philadelphia, a news-

Charlestown, Va, 2 December 1859.
I John Brown am now quite certain that the crimes of this guilty, land: will never be purged away; but with Blood: I had as I now think: vainly flattered myself that without very much bloodshed: it might be done

"John Brown's Last Prophecy," 1859
Chicago Historical Society

paperman observed, "She is just the woman to be the wife of the hero of Harpers Ferry. Stalwart of frame and strong in native intellect, she is imbued with the same religious faith, and her heart overflows with the same sympathies." In the light of that faith, she accepted the sentence of death by hanging with strength and fortitude. Indeed, as Brown told another late caller, "It had been decreed before the world was made."[25] Resignedly, the prisoner discountenanced efforts to rescue or reprieve him. Samuel Chilton, chief of Brown's counsel in succession to Botts, forwarded to Governor Wise a sheaf of affidavits pleading his insanity. Most of these documents seem to have been submitted to save the condemned man's life, and were discounted on that ground alone. But Wise, like Judge Parker, found no reason to question Brown's sanity.

The scaffold for the hanging of John Brown was erected in an open field on the edge of Charles Town. The "Fatal Friday," December 2, dawned bright. He was stoical, even cheerful, to the consternation of his guards. He had successfully turned his jail cell into his public stage. He seemed to be performing the last act of a heroic legend he had fashioned himself. He knew that he had fulfilled his mission and that martyrdom awaited him in death. He asked that no "hypocritical prayers" be said over him, and that he be attended to the scaffold only by "little, dirty, ragged, bare headed, and barefooted Slave boys and girls." He wore much the same clothes he had worn when captured: a tattered black suit, shirt, slouch hat, stockings, and boots. From his meager possessions he gave personal mementos to several guards. Before he left his cell he passed a message to one of them. "I John Brown am now quite *certain*," it read, "that the crimes of this *guilty land: will* never be purged *away;* but with Blood. I had *as I now think:* vainly flattered myself that without *very much* bloodshed; it might be done." Whether confession or prophecy or both, it was a powerful message. As he stepped from the porch of the jail, according to a report in the *New-York Tribune,* Brown saw a black woman holding a small child in her arms. "He stopped for a moment

"John Brown Ascending the Scaffold at Charles Town"

From Millard Kessler Bushong, *A History of Jefferson County, West Virginia* (Charles Town, W. Va., 1941)

in his course, stooped over, and with the tenderness of one whose love is as broad as the brotherhood of man, he kissed it affectionately." [26]

Helped into a wagon, he rode atop his own coffin behind a military escort the half-mile to the gallows with, it was said, "a forgiving smile" on his face. When one of the guards remarked on his coolness in the face of death, Brown said, "For thirty years I have been educated to look upon fear as a myth, and now I do not know what it is." Then, overlooking the countryside, he said, "What a beautiful country you have here." The execution, on Governor Wise's order, was a military proceeding closed to the public. Brown was disappointed not to see ordinary citizens about. A reporter for the *Baltimore Sun* had sneaked in under disguise. His description of the scene may be supplemented by the letter Colonel J. T. L. Preston, professor of Latin at the Virginia Military Institute, detailed to Charles Town, wrote to his wife. Troops of infantry and cavalry, nearly 3,000 in all, were drawn up in a hollow square around the platform with the gallows. It was, said Preston, "the greatest array of disciplined military force ever seen in Virginia." One of the soldiers, an actor attached to the Richmond Grays, had rushed from the theater in the capital where he was performing to witness the event. His name was John Wilkes Booth, and in his opinion old Brown was "a man inspired, the grandest character of the century," though a murderous traitor as well. Another witness, ludicrously yet significantly, was sixty-five-year-old Edmund Ruffin, editor, planter, and raving secessionist, who had slipped into the ranks with the connivance of the cadets. Brown's death was a red-letter day for the South, in Ruffin's opinion. Preston thought the condemned man's demeanor intrepid and dignified as the noose was put around his neck. "It was a moment of great solemnity." At 11:15 A.M. the trap opened. Brown's limp body hung for forty minutes before it was taken down.[27]

A month earlier the executive committee of the American Anti-Slavery Society had adopted a recommendation that the tragic event of Brown's death on the gallows should be observed on the day it occurred. And so it happened in many cities and towns from Boston to Cleveland and to Lawrence, Kansas. At Boston's crowded Tremont Temple, Garrison declared, "Today, Virginia has murdered John Brown; tonight we here witness his resurrection." (For weeks his newspaper had been assailing the statue of Daniel Webster, author of the Fugitive Slave Law, recently erected before the Massachusetts Statehouse.) In the afternoon at Concord, the people gathered at the Town Hall for an impressive service led by the Transcendentalist faithful. There were no speeches, only readings, poems, prayers, and hymns. Emerson, who spoke often during the John Brown epoch, had created a stir when he declared, like Child, that Brown's death "will make the gallows as glorious as the cross." His part in Concord's service was to read passages from Brown's speeches and letters. Having once remarked that "the highest virtue is always against the law," he readily, like Thoreau, saw Brown as a Transcendentalist saint. He was surprised to find himself in agreement with Governor Wise in praising Brown's courage. "Indeed, it is the *reductio ad absurdum* of Slavery," the philosopher wrote, "when the Governor of Virginia is forced to hang a man he declares to be a man of the most integrity, truthfulness, and courage he has ever met."[28] On Saturday, December 3, the *New-York Herald,* under the heading "Sympathy for John Brown in the North," ran five compact columns of small type to record the meetings across the country.

The crescendo came on Sunday, when Brown's witness to Christ was acclaimed in hundreds of churches. (Many congregants, of course, were opposed or silent.) From the pulpit of the Church of the Puritans in New York's Union Square, the Reverend George B. Cheever declared Brown a Christian hero and martyr. Striking a blow against Moloch, he was the first American to sacrifice his life for a race in bondage. A Methodist minister, Fales Henry Newhall, observed that the words "rebel" and "treason" were made holy by Brown's death. "Yes, henceforth it is no disgrace to die on a gibbet of this land." Moncure Conway, of the First Congregational Church in Cincinnati, had offended many of his parishioners by forthright defense of Brown's raid at Harpers Ferry; now he returned to the charge. His text revolved around an incident of the raid: the taking of a gold-handled sword belonging to Lewis Washington, great-grandnephew of George Washington, which Captain Brown had strapped to his waist and worn and wielded until his capture. This was no ordinary sword. It was a gift of Frederick the Great to the victorious general of the American Revolution and was inscribed, "From the oldest general in the world to the greatest." Dwelling on the symbolism, which had not escaped the captain, Conway said, "If the spirit of Washington could still rule in our land, I believe it would have presented that sword to John Brown as its rightful in-

THE JOHN BROWN EPOCH 25

heritor with the words: "From the greatest general in the world to the purest."[29]

Needless to say, John Brown was a compelling subject for poets. "The Second of December 1859!" Henry Wadsworth Longfellow exclaimed. "The date of the New Revolution: quite as much needed as the old one." Young William Dean Howells, in Ohio, lauded the old lion tangled in the "ghostly gallows-tree":

Death kills not. In a later time
  (O slow, but all-accomplishing!)
    Thy shouted name abroad shall ring,
Wherever right makes war sublime.

In "The Virginia Scaffold," Edna Dean Proctor dwelled upon the image of the crucified hero:

They may hang him on the gibbet; they may raise the victor's cry,
When they see him darkly swinging like a speck against the sky;
Ah, the dying of a hero, that the right may win the way,
Is but sowing seed for harvest in a warm and mellow May!
Now his story shall be whispered by the firelight's evening glow
And in fields of rice and cotton, when the hot noon passes slow,
Till his name shall be a watchword from Missouri to the sea,
And the planting finds its reaping in the birthday of the Free![30]

Not all the poems were so solemn. Edmund Stedman's "How Old Brown Took Harper's Ferry" is a rollicking verse narrative of that foray and the trial, with a punchy ending.

How he spoke his grand oration, in the scorn of all denial;
  What the brave old madman told them,—these are known the
    country o'er.
      'Hang Old Brown
      Osawatomie Brown,'
Said the judge, 'and all such rebels!' with his most judicial frown.

But, Virginians, don't do it! for I tell you that the flagon,
   Filled with blood of Old Brown's offspring, was first poured by
      Southern hands;
And each drop from Old Brown's life-veins, like the red gore of the
   dragon,
   May spring up a vengeful Fury, hissing through your slave-worn
      lands!
      And Old Brown,
      Osawatomie Brown,
May trouble you more than ever, when you've nailed his coffin
   down![31]

The most important of the many poems was John Greenleaf Whittier's "Brown of Osawatomie," first published in the *Independent*. Whittier was an observant Quaker and abolitionist, indeed widely celebrated as the foremost antislavery poet. He, too, imagined the dying hero, as if in acknowledgment that John Brown's death was more important than his life. Dwelling on his last day, the poet begins with Brown saying:

"I will not have, to shrive my soul, a priest in slavery's pay
But let some poor slave mother whom I have striven to free,
With her children, from the gallows-stair
Put up a prayer for me!"

Whittier then picks up the story from the *Tribune:*

And he stooped between the jeering ranks
And kissed the negro child!

Adding:

The shadows of his stormy life that moment fell apart;
And they who blamed the bloody hand forgave the loving heart.

But here the halo is dimmed: "Perish with him the folly that seeks through evil good!"

O! Never may young blue-ridged hills the Northern rifle hear,
Nor see the light of blazing homes flash on the negro's spear.[32]

The poet's Quakerism overrode his abolitionist's admiration for John Brown.

William Lloyd Garrison, the *Liberator*'s editor, nailed Whittier for turning his tribute into moral censure. Garrison, while not a Quaker, adhered to the same nonresistance principles and had nevertheless justified Brown's resort to force. "Our views of war and bloodshed are well known . . . ," he wrote. "But let no one who glories in the Revolutionary struggle of 1776 deny the rights of slaves to imitate the example of our fathers." He thought Brown wrongheaded, yet his moral purpose was totally in accord with the principles of the Revolution. Whittier, too, in many of his poems had gloried in the battles of Lexington, Bunker Hill, and Yorktown. Still he faulted Brown for "guilty means"—"the rash and bloody hand." The censure was invidious, even hateful, said Garrison. The poet replied in self-defense, and the editor rejoined that John Brown, in losing his life to free the slaves, acted in the spirit of General Joseph Warren and other worthies of 1776. For many abolitionists Brown's example resolved the troubling issue between moral suasion and righteous violence well before the war came.[33]

The northern salute upon the death of John Brown—the tolling bells, firing of minute guns, hymns of praise—was met with astonishment and dismay in the South. In weighing the effects of Harpers Ferry on the southern mind, it is imperative to distinguish between the raid, which was a small affair, and the northern response to it, which roared like thunder across the South. Perhaps no event better demonstrated the impact than the "secession" of southern medical students from Philadelphia. Every year hundreds of medical students flocked to Philadelphia: Jefferson Medical College alone took over 60 percent of its enrollment from southern states. Brown's execution was observed by a noon prayer vigil in the city's National Hall. The proceedings were interrupted by a group of rowdies sending up cheers for Governor Wise. Tempers escalated several days later when the Pennsylvania Anti-Slavery Society held its annual convention and fair in the city. Speakers were harried by catcalls from riotous southern students; police were summoned and sixteen persons were arrested. A Virginian, Hunter McGuire, later to distinguish himself as Stonewall Jackson's surgeon, felt he was in "enemy's country." On December 20 several hundred alienated medical students met and voted a resolution to "secede." The next day 257 of them marched in a body to the railroad station and boarded a train for Richmond. On their arrival, a band serenaded them with "Carry Me Back to Old Virginia." They were also lampooned in the northern press as "the Medical Lighthearted Brigade," with apologies to Tennyson:

> Right from the jaws of Death
> Rushed the mad sectionalists—
> Wretched dissectionists,
>   All out of breath;
> Letting the fee go, down to the depot
>   Rushed they—two hundred!
>   Medical sawbones all—
>   Heedless jawbones all—
>   Thinking of rawbones all!
> "Curse the North!" was their cry—
>   Theirs not to reason why,
>   But like young colts to shie,
>   Lest the grim ghost of Brown
>   Tumble the Union down!
>   Oh, funny two hundred![34]

While the trials of Brown's criminal associates continued in Charles Town—and northern friends fretted over rescue attempts—the hero himself was buried in North Elba. His body was delivered to Mrs. Brown the evening of December 2. With it she set out the next morning by way of Baltimore, Philadelphia, New York, and Troy, thence across Lake Champlain to Westport, finally to the

Adirondack home. The Reverend Joshua Young, a Unitarian minister from Burlington, Vermont, had volunteered to make the hazardous journey and to consecrate the grave. He later recalled the scene.

> All around stood the deep primeval forest bending to the western winds, while in the near distance, capped with snow, loomed the everlasting hills, grand and solemn, mingling the sublimity of nature with the moral grandeur of an immortal deed. It was the old, old story of a prophet's fate, "Truth forever on the scaffold, wrong forever on the throne."

Wendell Phillips, who had attended Mary Brown on her journey home, eulogized the fallen lion. He had abolished slavery in Virginia, the orator said. "Insurrection was a harsh, horrid word to millions a month ago. John Brown went a whole generation beyond it, claiming the right of the white man to help the slave to freedom by arms." The service at the grave closed as the mourners sang the martyr's favorite hymn:

> Blow ye the trumpet blow!
> The gladly solemn sound.
> Let all the nations know
> To earth's remotest bound,
> The glory of jubilee to come.[35]

The John Brown epoch came to a close amid a wave of reaction voiced at Union meetings in northern cities. They were often boisterous. The question of the hour was "Should the Union be preserved?" Edward Everett, the splendid Unionist orator, held Brown's character up to ridicule and evoked the horrors of Santo Domingo and "a half-caste Republic." Congress, meanwhile, came into session. There random debate on Brown and disunion was short-circuited by the Senate's adoption of a resolution to appoint a select committee of inquiry into the Harpers Ferry invasion. Senator Mason, of Virginia, was named chairman, and four others—two from each section and party—were appointed. The committee proceeded deliberately over six months, taking testimony from persons who had known or encountered Brown and his associates before and during events culminating in the raid. Some of the testimony threw light on Brown's motives and purposes. Andrew Hunter, the prosecutor, referred to a letter Brown had written to him denying insurrectionary intentions. He meant rather, said Brown, "to place the slaves in a condition to defend their liberties, if they would, without any bloodshed, but not that I intended to run them out of the slave states." William F. M. Arny, the New York agent of the Kansas Aid Committee, with whom Brown had talked of his ambitious plans, said he aimed to create such havoc in the mountains of the slave states as to cause the whole system to collapse. He was, said Arny, contemptuous of "the do-nothing policy of the abolitionists." Charles Robinson, the Kansas leader, thought Brown intended to use his operations in Kansas as a springboard to wider disturbance in the Union. Richard Realf, an English journalist in Kansas, was also privy to Brown's design in Virginia. He told a revealing anecdote of the warrior's attitude toward blacks. When one of them, traveling with his party, was denied accommodation at a hotel, Brown stomped out and went elsewhere.[36]

Testimony of the Secret Six was awaited with special interest. The Senate committee was disappointed, however. Of the six, Parker was near death in Rome, Smith pleaded temporary insanity, Sanborn defied the committee, and Higginson was never called. Both Howe and Stearns testified, admitting to vague knowledge of Brown's plan to strike somewhere along the Virginia border, but swearing that they knew neither where or when. Stearns said that had he known more earlier, he would have disapproved and perhaps intervened. Now, however, months after the event, he was of a different mind. "I believe," he said, "John Brown to be the representative man of this century, as Washington was of the last." Stearns, a wealthy Massachusetts manufacturer and abolitionist, also testified to Brown's enigmatic manner by recalling his answer when a Kansas aid committee asked him whether he intended to invade a slave state: "I am no adventurer; you all know me. . . . I do not expose my plans; no one knows them but myself. . . . I do not wish to be interrogated; if you wish to give me anything, I want you to give it freely. I have no other purpose but to serve the cause of liberty."[37]

The Senate committee reported on June 15, 1860. "There can be no doubt," it concluded, "that Brown's plan was to commence servile war on the border of Virginia, which he expected to extend . . . throughout the entire South." But the committee could not prove this charge; nor did it have anything to recommend to Congress. It had, in its course, jailed one person, Thaddeus Hyatt, who violated a subpoena to testify. Hyatt had made himself obnoxious to the committee by his efforts to aid the Brown family.[38]

The John Brown epoch faded and the disunion epoch began in earnest with the presidential election. In February 1860 Abraham Lincoln, Illinois's candidate for the Republican nomination, introduced himself to eastern audiences with an important speech at the Cooper Union in New York. He had come forward in 1854 as a vigorous opponent of "popular sovereignty" in Kansas and had followed closely the struggle for freedom in the territory. He never met John Brown; he went to Kansas in the fall of 1859, after the raid at Harpers Ferry. In his speeches there he said the attack was wrong, first because it was against the law and second because it was futile. "John Brown has shown great courage, rare unselfishness, as even Gov. Wise testifies. But no man, North or South, can approve of violence or crime." In New York he took pains to lift the imputation of the crime from the Republican Party. (He probably understood, however, that the imputation fell mainly on the head of the front-running candidate, William H. Seward, and so improved his own prospects.) "Harper's Ferry! John Brown!!" he exclaimed in exasperation. "John Brown was no Republican." Nor had the Senate committee implicated a single Republican politician in his enterprise. Brown was a zealot who believed himself commissioned by Heaven to liberate the slaves. Republicans, by contrast, believed in the Union and the Constitution. In the future Lincoln would have occasion to think that he, too, "might be an instrument in God's hands" for the same purpose.[39] The turn Brown gave to slaveholders' fears set the mind of the South upon secession should Lincoln or any other Republican candidate be elected president. Curiously, Edmund Ruffin, the Virginia oracle of disunion, who had exulted in Harpers Ferry and witnessed Brown's hanging, pulled the lanyard of the cannon that fired the first shot in the Civil War, though some Confederates came to say that, in truth, the first shot was fired by John Brown at Harpers Ferry.[40]

2

Faces and Places of the Hero

I N 1 8 6 5, after General Lee surrendered at Appomattox, after President Lincoln was assassinated, the Concord sage, Emerson, wrote in his journal, "It has been impossible to keep the name of John Brown out of the war from first to last." His tormentors were forgotten, "but John Brown's soul is marching on." [1] The John Brown song resonated to the marching feet of Union soldiers and the roar of Union cannon from the early months of the war. Accounts vary slightly, but the song seems to have originated in the 12th Regiment of Massachusetts Volunteer Infantry, stationed that spring at Fort Warren, in Boston Harbor. Four of the sergeants formed a quartet. Among their favorite airs was "Say, Brothers, Will You Meet Us," popular with Methodists, to which they wished to set appropriately martial words. The remembered tragedy at Charles Town, Virginia, combined with their good-natured banter with the sergeant whose name was John Brown, led spontaneously to the first verse:

> John Brown's body lies a-mouldering in the grave
> But his soul goes marching on.

Four more verses followed, each separated by the refrain, "Glory, glory, hallelujah!" At once a favorite with the soldiers, the song was taken up by the regimental band and played at dress parade on Boston Common. Bound southward in July, the Massachusetts 12th,

commanded by Fletcher Webster, son of the statesman, marched
down New York's Broadway to the strains of "John Brown's Body." It
would henceforth be known as the Hallelujah Regiment.[2]

Soon, of course, the song was heard everywhere. New verses
touching the martyr's life were introduced; for instance:

> He captured Harper's Ferry, with his minute men so few,
> And frightened Old Virginny 'til she trembled thru and thru;
> They hung him for a traitor, themselves a traitor crew,
> But his soul is marching on.
>   Glory, glory, hallelujah![3]

Not only did the song become a war anthem, it gave birth to the national psalm "The Battle Hymn of the Republic," by Julia Ward
Howe. As Mrs. Samuel Gridley Howe she had met and entertained
John Brown in her Boston home. Upon his death, she had written,
"I should be glad to be as sure of heaven as that old man may be."
In the fall of 1861 Mrs. Howe accompanied her husband and several friends to Washington. Returning in their carriage from a military review, the group burst into the song everyone was singing;
and James Freeman Clarke, her ministerial friend, remarked, "Mrs.
Howe, why do you not write some words for that stirring tune?" She,
an aspiring poet, took the thought to bed with her, and the next
morning, at dawn, the words came, line by line, stanza by stanza,
"sweeping on with the rhythm of the marching feet." Springing out
of bed, she reached for a pen and wrote it all down. Published in
the *Atlantic Monthly* the following February, it created a sensation.[4]
In its message, as in its music, it was kindred to John Brown and
his song.

> Mine eyes have seen the glory of the coming of the Lord:
> He is trampling out the vintage where the grapes of wrath are
>   stored;
> He hath loosed the fateful lightning by his terrible swift sword:
> His truth is marching on.

Soldiers in gray made their own version of the song, which threatened to hang the Yanks in old Charles Town. Some years later, Murat Halstead, who had witnessed Brown's hanging, heard it sung in German by the spike-helmeted invaders in Lorraine during the Franco-Prussian War.

Six of the captain's men followed him to the gallows. One was twenty-four-year-old Edwin Coppoc, whose younger brother, Barclay, escaped. Both were Quakers from Springdale, Iowa; both were "disowned," it was said, after the raid at Harpers Ferry. When Edwin's body returned home, a family friend, Daniel Bonsall, wrote to Governor Wise denouncing "the wilful murder of some of the best men that have graced the pages of History," signing himself, "Thine Respectfully," then adding, "We shall not bury Edwin Coppich [*sic*] in the Virginia Coffin but would be rejoiced if her governor would come or send for it." By this time John Letcher had become governor of the commonwealth; and he made strenuous efforts to extradite the younger Coppoc for trial, without success. The fugitive from justice, meanwhile, undertook to organize John Brown Leagues dedicated to carrying on the hero's work. Abolitionist anger and dissent were swirling through Ohio's Western Reserve. The league was a secret society sometimes known as the Black Strings, after the insignia worn in the buttonhole of the shirt. When the war came, Coppoc was commissioned a lieutenant in the Third Kansas Volunteer Infantry under Colonel James Montgomery, earlier an intrepid comrade of John Brown. In 1861, unhappily, Barclay Coppoc lost his life on a train that plunged into the Little Platte River. When the war ended, in Salem, Ohio, where the Coppoc brothers were born and where Edwin was buried, the infamous Virginia metal coffin was hauled out for a victory celebration. An effigy of General Lee was laid in it and the coffin was carried on the backs of Union soldiers at the head of the procession marching to the hallelujahs of "John Brown's Body" in what a historian has deftly called "an exhibit of the compensatory justice of history." The relic was later added to the collection of the Ohio Historical Society.[5]

Oberlin, Ohio, meanwhile, mourned three of its own, all blacks: John A. Copeland, Lewis Sheridan Leary, and Shields Green, the first two having been students in the college. One of the professors, James Monroe, on behalf of Copeland's parents, traveled to Virginia in December to recover their son's body. Monroe discovered it had been spirited away by medical students. Leary's body, too, had been offered up to medical science. Monroe came back with but one body, that of the little-known Green, who had chosen to accompany Brown when his friend Frederick Douglass would not. Funeral services were held for these three victims of Harpers Ferry on Christmas Day, 1859. Six years later a cenotaph was erected in Oberlin to the three black victims.[6]

The unfolding events of the war slowly crowded out the place John Brown had held in the consciousness of the American people. The commemoration of Martyr's Day, December 2, faded in antislavery circles. On that day in 1861, a mob broke up the evening memorial service at Tremont Temple in Boston. Only the heartiest champions, such as the black minister Henry Highland Garnet, persevered. William Lloyd Garrison's pilgrimage to John Brown's grave in the Adirondacks was news in 1862; and there were occasional wafts of sympathy for John Brown's widow and eight surviving children. Thaddeus Hyatt, in efforts for their relief, offered a fine photograph of John Brown in exchange for a dollar donation. Three thousand were reportedly subscribed. Who can guess in how many homes his portrait was hung? On a Sunday during the first year of the war Henry Ward Beecher walked into his pulpit at Brooklyn's Plymouth Church with the shackles and chains that had bound John Brown at Charles Town. How he acquired them was unclear, but presumably these relics of martyrdom moved the congregation. The president's promulgation of the Emancipation Proclamation on January 1, 1863, reminded many abolitionists of the nation's debt to John Brown. As Victor Hugo had predicted, "What the South slew . . . was not John Brown but slavery."[7] Garnet held a midnight vigil at the Shiloh

Church in New York. In his sermon he reiterated the prophecy of John Brown: "For the sins of this nation there is no atonement without the shedding of blood." The Emancipation Proclamation was his vindication. At the Massachusetts Statehouse Governor John A. Andrew, who had famously declared on the hero's death that, regardless of the rightness or wrongness of his effort, "John Brown himself was right," paraded around his office singing the "Hallelujah Song."[8]

Harpers Ferry, the place apart from the event, became a battleground, and so was not forgotten. On April 16, four days after the bombardment of Fort Sumter, Virginia troops captured Harpers Ferry with no more authority than John Brown had had, but without loss of life. The commonwealth's ordinance of secession followed. Of course, as Brown had learned, the place was indefensible. Oddly, Hector Tyndale, one of the Philadelphians who had accompanied Mrs. Brown to retrieve her husband's body at Harpers Ferry, found himself in command, twenty-six months later, of the 28th Pennsylvania Infantry, which burned the arsenal. Troops both Blue and Gray swept through Harpers Ferry for four years. "The whole village is a mass of ruins," a Massachusetts cavalryman observed in July 1862. Several years after the war, the reporter G. A. Townsend, whose pseudonym was Gath, wrote of the place: "It is a village of paupers who hang upon the approaching sale by the United States of the armory and arsenal grounds as their last and vital chance of existence." As for nearby Charles Town, it, too, was "a place accursed."[9]

After Appomattox and the collapse of the Confederacy, many northerners who had never hurrahed for Brown or who perhaps blamed him for the fiery ordeal could no longer withhold a measure of admiration. Who ever thought, a sober New Yorker mused, that John Brown would march so fast? "What a *nunc dimittis* would the valiant old man have sung under the gallows tree had he foreseen the day."[10] One of the delicious ironies of the John Brown legend concerned Henry A. Wise, the former governor who became a Confederate general and whose plantation in Princess Anne County was ravaged by the war. The head of the restored government, meeting Wise in Richmond after it fell to the Union in 1865, heard how upon returning to the plantation Wise had entered the dilapidated manor house. "And what do you suppose I found there?" he asked the governor, Francis Pierpont. "Why, sir, I found John Brown's daughter teaching a negro school in my mansion." Wise gave no name, but the teacher may have been one of the two daughters Franklin B. Sanborn had brought to his school in Concord. As in a trance, the former governor, who had known in his heart that "the idol of slavery" would be destroyed only by fire and blood, mused calmly, "'John Brown was a great man, sir; he was a great man. Yes,' he added, raising his right hand and assuming a majestic attitude, 'John Brown was a hero; John Brown was a hero, sir!'"[11]

• • JOHN BROWN made an inauspicious entrance into literature, apart from eulogy and panegyric, in a melodrama, *Ossawatomie Brown, or The Insurrection at Harper's Ferry*, at the Bowery Theatre, New York, December 16, 1859. The author, Mrs. J. C. Swayze, wrote a "tableaux play" in three acts and fifteen scenes. It opens upon Mrs. Brown, at North Elba, pondering the imminent wedding of her son Frederick, then shifts to Kansas and dramatizes Frederick's death and his father's oath of revenge at Osawatomie. In Act III, at Kennedy Farm, Brown mulls over his plan of attack and scoffs at Douglass's withdrawal: "There's a wet blanket, and from a professed abolitionist!" It proceeds to the fight at the Engine House, and closes with Brown's surrender. As bad as the play was, it established the basic scenario of the stage John Brown.[12]

Reporters began to assemble the pieces of Brown's life from the first news of events at Harpers Ferry. An eyewitness account, *A Voice from Harpers Ferry*, by one of the raiders who escaped, Osborn P. Anderson, a free black from Canada, was published early in 1861. It offered tantalizing glimpses of the Captain at the climax of his life.

Much more important, however, was the first biography, *The Public Life of Capt. John Brown,* which appeared the same year.

Its author, James Redpath, was a Scottish-born abolitionist and journalist who encountered Brown in Kansas. As a reporter for the *New-York Tribune,* Redpath had earlier made three journeys in the South to obtain inside knowledge of the slaves' condition and mental outlook. His clandestine interviews with bondsmen were published in northern antislavery newspapers under the alias John Ball Jr. In 1855 Redpath went to Kansas, which he called the Lexington and Concord of "the second American revolution." Four years later he dedicated his book *The Roving Editor; or Talks with Slaves,* to Captain John Brown: "To you, old Hero, I dedicate the record of my Talks with the Slaves in the Southern States." And he went on to laud the hero's dauntless bravery, his belief in the blacks, and his insurrectionary spirit.[13]

Redpath did not disguise the hagiographic character of his biography. It was, in a sense, authorized by the family, who shared the royalties equally with the author. With comparatively little research and an assist from other reporters, such as Richard Hinton, Redpath constructed his story from the public record, personal acquaintance, family tradition, and abundant letters, many heretofore unpublished. He accepted without question the family lore that John Brown was the sixth descendant of Peter Brown, who came to Plymouth on the *Mayflower* in 1620. For the hero's early life Redpath relied on the autobiographical letter penned for young Frank P. Stearns, the son of George and Mary Stearns, the dearest of Brown's Boston friends, which took him to his twenty-first year. The family record was carefully laid out: twenty children by two wives, born between 1821 and 1854. But persons and places, influences and events were roughly charted. To account for a character so remarkable, "a stern inflexibility of purpose, and an earnestness of nature so intense that it did not seem to exist,—as wheels that revolve with the velocity of lightning, hardly seem to the looker-on to be moving at all," Redpath under-

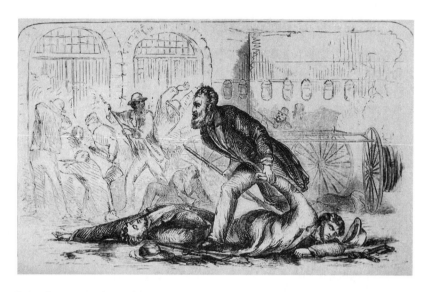

John Brown and his dying sons

From James Redpath, *The Public Life of Capt. John Brown* (Boston, 1860)

scored the power of biblical Christianity on Brown. "He was the last of the old Puritan type of Christians. Gideon, to him, and Joshua, and Moses, were not interesting historic characters merely . . . but holy examples set before us, by Deity himself, for our imitation and guidance." In youth he had hoped to go to Amherst College and become a minister of the Gospel. This hope was not realized, however, in part because of his restive nature; and his education was sporadic at best. Redpath alluded to favorite books, secular and religious. Brown admired Cromwell, Washington, and Napoleon, and had a rough acquaintance with European and American history. It was well known that he had been a failure in business. Redpath, while he acknowledged as much, pointed up "his perfect integrity of character" and traced the difficulty to "that same spirit of resistance to organized wrong" that had distinguished his forebears, evinced so well in his hostility to slavery. The parties responsible for his failure as a wool grower and trader were the New England manufacturers who had conspired against him.[14]

The author traced Brown's fierce moral commitment to liberation of the slaves back to 1839. Thereafter the antislavery cause trespassed upon his business affairs. As partner in the Ohio firm of Perkins & Brown, he used the opportunity of a business trip to London to tour battlefields in Europe for knowledge they might shed on guerrilla warfare in the southern Appalachians. Brown's move to North Elba, in the Adirondacks, pretty much ended his business life; and, of course, his life was driven substantially by his concern for fugitive slaves. In 1854 the first of the great fugitive-slave rescue cases, the Anthony Burns case, occurred in Boston. At that time Brown was a defendant in a suit for recovery of debt in Troy, New York. Redpath repeated an anecdote that had appeared in the press after the raid in Virginia. The next morning, it seems, Brown rose from breakfast and announced to his attorney, "I am going to Boston." "What!" said the astonished lawyer. "Why do you want to go to Boston?" and Brown replied, "Anthony Burns must be released, or I will die in the attempt." Counsel remonstrated, pointing out that they were so far the victors in this suit, which was on appeal, and Brown grudgingly repressed his zeal.[15]

When Kansas opened up, Brown was quick to follow his sons there. Kansas was the next battleground in his private war against slavery. Redpath said he first encountered Brown in Osawatomie, in 1855, at a caucus of free-state settlers on a resolution that dedicated Kansas to free white labor only. Alarmed and disgusted, the newcomer spoke vigorously against the resolution and acclaimed the humanity of black people. "This was John Brown's first and last appearance in a public meeting in Kansas," Redpath observed. He characterized Brown's warrior-like acts as "exclusively defensive." Of the Pottawatomie Massacre, in which five pro-slavery men lost their lives, still little known to history, Redpath said Brown was falsely accused, and described the killing as "one of those stern acts of summary justice with which the history of the West and every civil war

Bust of John Brown,
Edwin A. Brackett, 1863
Boston Athenaeum

abounds." He called the Battle of Osawatomie "one of the most brilliant episodes of Kansas history," from which the Missourians never recovered, and named Brown its hero.[16]

The latter half of Redpath's biography turns on Harpers Ferry. It was the consummate act of Brown's life. His comings and goings between Kansas and the East from 1857 to 1859 are but lightly treated, although the chapters on recruitment and training of a small strike force at Tabor, Iowa, and the formation of a constitution for a provisional government at Chatham, Canada West, added to the knowledge of these subjects. Since the constitution premised a temporary government of freed slaves, it tended to sustain Brown's disavowal of an intention to run off liberated slaves to the North. The raid, the trial, and the hanging, of course, were still fresh in the public mind. Redpath's account added little to newspaper reports. He held that Captain Brown's delay in making his escape from the arsenal proved fatal to his plan. The failure, in sum, was not in the plan but in the execution. Many analysts to come would agree with this assessment.

As a by-product of his biography, Redpath edited a valuable collection, *Echoes of Harper's Ferry,* surveying the northern response. *The Public Life of Capt. John Brown* went through countless editions. Other prospective biographers, such as Lydia Maria Child, backed off before it. Redpath enjoyed an active and productive life for another thirty-one years. He promoted black emigration to Haiti, served as superintendent of schools in Charleston, South Carolina, during Reconstruction, and, most significantly, directed a successful lyceum. Despite the biography's success, Redpath never returned to the subject of John Brown. Nor did he ever regret his devotion to him, his family, and his cause.

• • IN BOSTON the Emancipation Proclamation, January 1, 1863, was celebrated at the Music Hall by a "Jubilee Concert." Afterward Mr. and Mrs. Stearns played host to a select group of friends at their home, Evergreens, in nearby Medford, to witness the unveiling of a bust of John Brown by the self-taught sculptor Edwin A. Brackett. The Stearnses had commissioned the work and hastily dispatched Brackett to Charles Town to take the condemned hero's features. Wendell Phillips spoke that evening; Emerson repeated his "Boston Hymn," and Harriet Beecher Stowe, author of *Uncle Tom's Cabin,* recited "The Battle Hymn of the Republic." The bust drew enthusiastic praise. Sanborn wrote a sonnet on it. Some observers, then and later, saw a resemblance to Michelangelo's *Moses.* Redpath, who later viewed it in the Boston Athenaeum, where it was exhibited among the busts of Roman emperors, thought the man portrayed might be Moses but it certainly was not John Brown.[17]

Stearns, one of the Secret Six, had been the most generous contributor to Brown's last campaign. "I consider it the proudest act of

my life that I gave good old John Brown every pike and rifle he carried to Harpers Ferry," he declared.[18] During the war Stearns worked
with Governor John Andrew to organize the first black infantry regiment, the 54th Massachusetts, under Colonel Robert Gould Shaw.
Together the two abolitionists thrilled at the regiment's marching to
"John Brown's Body" over ground where Crispus Attucks had bled
before the Revolution and from which Anthony Burns had been
hauled back into slavery. Another of the six, Thomas Wentworth
Higginson, organized and commanded a black regiment at Port
Royal, South Carolina. James Montgomery, Brown's Kansas comrade, raised a black regiment in the Rebel State.

At Beaufort, among the Sea Islands, where Charlotte Forten and
the other Yankee schoolmistresses taught the children to sing the
"Hallelujah song," some of them would also learn the story of the
martyr's kissing a black child before ascending the scaffold. Mrs.
Child included the story in the *Freedmen's Book*, which she edited for
use in the freedmen's schools. The title of her seven-stanza poem,
first published in the *Liberator* as "The Hero's Heart" in 1860, was
changed to "John Brown and the Colored Child" in this book. Beginning with the third stanza, it reads:

> The old man met no friendly eye,
> When last he looked on earth and sky;
> But one small child with timid air,
> Was gazing on his hoary hair.
>
> As that dark brow of his upturned,
> The tender heart within him yearned;
> And, fondly stooping o'er her face,
> He kissed her for her injured race.
>
> The little one she knew not why
> That kind old man went forth to die;
> Nor why, 'mid all the pomp and stir,
> He stooped to give a kiss to *her*.

But Jesus smiled that sight to see,
And said, "He did it unto *me*."
The golden harps then sweetly rung,
And this the song the angels sung:

"Who loves the poor doth love the Lord;
Earth cannot dim thy bright reward;
We hover o'er yon gallows high,
And wait to bear thee to the sky." [19]

The story, with its Christlike adumbrations, found an enduring
place in John Brown lore. Redpath embroidered it in his account of
the hero's "victory over death." "As he passed along," he wrote, "a
black woman with a child in her arms, ejaculated, 'God bless you, old
man; I wish I could help you, but I cannot.'" [20] In some variants, the
blessing occurs at the gallows' stairs. At least three artists painted the
kissing scene. The earliest, Louis Ransom, painted a black Madonna
and Child before the martyr. Exhibited in P. T. Barnum's Museum
in New York in 1863, it was distasteful, even blasphemous, to some
viewers, and city officials ordered it removed. Some years later Ransom presented the painting to Oberlin College. The most famous of
these renditions, *The Last Moments of John Brown,* was the work of
Thomas Hovenden in 1884. Often reproduced, it was joined by Cur-
rier and Ives lithographs after these paintings. Many Victorian man-
telpieces were graced with the touching scene. [21]

In 1882 an enterprising reporter in Louisville claimed he had located the child Brown had kissed, James Williams, now an adult.
Williams's mother said she had met "Massa" Brown years earlier,
possibly when he was employed as a surveyor in the Alleghenies. "He
taught me to read and write, and give me this little Bible." She was
one of the first to go to him in Charles Town jail; and on the day of
the execution she went there with her baby, "and he just looked at me
in the kind of way he had with us niggers and tried to lay his hand
on my head, but couldn't on account of the ropes, and he muttered
suthin' in a low tone. Then I held up Jim there, and he put his face

right down and kissed this little nigger on his forehead. And then he just walked right up to the scaffold and made his little speech. You oughter seen how the crowd cried." The falsity of the conclusion casts doubt on the truthfulness of the whole. Other reporters found other claimants to John Brown's benediction, in Memphis and in Charles Town.[22]

Over the years the famous kiss was discredited by several sources. First, Captain John Avis, Brown's kindly jailer, who had accompanied him to the scaffold, denied that anything of the sort happened, or could have happened because of the shackles the prisoner wore. Second, Edward F. Underhill, the erstwhile *Tribune* correspondent, said he had written the story in the New York office from secondhand reports. An alternate attribution was to the *Tribune*'s Henry S. Olcott.[23] Whether the story was fact or fiction, many people believed it because they believed John Brown was a martyr for the black people. The kiss, moreover, was perfectly in keeping with the doomed man's sympathetic character. As a contemporary, George P. Putnam, wrote:

> Great God! that kiss—its thrilling hath not perished.
>   But on from clime to clime
> Leaping from heart to heart, it shall be cherished
>   Till the last impulse of Time![24]

In 1928 the Reverend William E. Barton, well known for his studies of Abraham Lincoln, graciously accepted the gift of a copy of Ransom's painting for the Lake Placid Club, near John Brown's resting place. Declaring that the story of the kiss was an imperishable part of the John Brown tradition, he went on curiously, "In some respects it may be more true than the bald historic fact would have been."[25]

Benjamin Quarles, the African American historian, has said that the idea of John Brown as hero and martyr was held most fervently by blacks. Indeed, the opinion that he "ranks among the world's greatest heroes" was authoritatively asserted by the country's first African American historian, George Washington Williams, in 1882.

The Last Moments of John Brown, Thomas Hovenden, 1884
The Metropolitan Museum of Art, New York; gift of Mr. and Mrs. Carl Stoeckel, 1897

Brown was the John the Baptist of black freedom. "John Brown is rapidly settling down to his proper place in history, and 'the madman' has been transformed into a 'saint.'"[26] In this view Williams was warmly supported by two long-lived black abolitionists: Frederick Douglass and Henry Highland Garnet. The latter, a tall dark man with a limp, was well known for his early advocacy of forcible black resistance to slavery. "Rather die free men than live to be slaves," he had declared in a notable address in 1843. This sentiment endeared him to John Brown but was gently opposed by Douglass. Reputedly the most eloquent of black orators, Garnet was invited to address Congress upon the adoption of the Thirteenth Amendment, the highest honor ever paid to a black citizen. Some years later, in 1878, his Shiloh Church unveiled a memorial bust of John Brown, the work of Edmonia Lewis, a black sculptor known for *The Dying Cleopatra* and similar works. Garnet, at the reception on this occasion, let his mind wander back to his last conversation with the martyred hero. "Friend Brown, it seems to me that there is not much hope for the success of the work you are about to undertake." And Brown replied:

> "Friend Garnet, you may be right . . . but I believe that God has sent me to do what I may, and if I die in the attempt I shall know that I have done right, and that thousands shall rise to take my place!" He was right. . . . I never knew a man who was better acquainted with Scripture than John Brown. He never swore, he never drank a drop of intoxicating liquor, and never used tobacco. He was a man of strict morality and a lover of religion.

The service was concluded with the hymn "Blow Ye the Trumpet, Blow," a reading from the hero's letters, and the singing of "John Brown's Body."[27]

In the years after the war Frederick Douglass could never quite decide whether to apologize or to give thanks for his decision not to join John Brown at Harpers Ferry. The full measure of devotion he withheld from Abraham Lincoln—"We are at best his stepchildren," he had said on a great occasion—he did not withhold from Brown. Douglass reviewed the subject in "John Brown: An Address on the Fourteenth Anniversary of Storer College," in 1881. The college, at Harpers Ferry, had been established for the education of black men and found its campus among the abandoned arsenal's Engine House and other buildings where Brown had briefly held forth in October 1859. A virtual industry in John Brown memorabilia sprang up in Harpers Ferry after the war. Douglass's lecture was the most significant event in the history of the struggling college. Andrew J. Hunter, the state's attorney who had prosecuted Brown, sat on the platform. (The ceremony concluded, he invited Douglass to Charles Town, but the orator declined.) Douglass extolled the martyr: "His zeal for the cause was far greater than mine—it was the burning sun to my taper light." He spoke without regret of his decision at Chambersburg. He addressed some unanswered questions about the raid. He left no doubt of his reverence for Captain Brown. He it was, said Douglass, "who began the war that ended American slavery and made this a free Republic. Until this blow was struck, the prospect for freedom was dim, shadowy, and uncertain. . . . When John Brown stretched forth his arm the sky was cleared."[28]

•• T H E J O H N B R O W N legend's most sacred spot is the grave where the hero lies buried in North Elba, New York. His widow, Mary, with a houseful of children and grandchildren, lived there for about four years after the funeral. Mary and most of the family finally drifted to California. She settled first with a daughter who taught school at Red Bluff, on the Sacramento River. An editorial in the *New York Times* reported that they were impoverished and sent out a plea for aid. The report was immediately denied, however. Eight children survived their father's death. The oldest, John Brown Jr., lived in Put-In-Bay, Ohio, where he grew grapes and, with other interests, minded his father's reputation. Almost anything touching the family was news, because, and only because, they were the martyr's children. Ruth, the oldest daughter, was an occasional correspondent in the press. Owen, who miraculously escaped with his life, lived for a time in Ohio, then went to California, where he resided with his brother Jason in a hilltop cabin above Pasadena. He died in 1889, the last survivor of the raid. In 1875 William Lloyd Garrison, on behalf of a committee of French savants led by Victor Hugo, presented a gold medal to Mrs. Brown and the children. (It was delayed several years by the Franco-Prussian War.) A handsome work, the medal was embellished with a conjectured head of Brown in bas relief and suitably inscribed on the back.

In 1882 Mrs. Brown, having moved to Santa Clara County, made a return trip to the East on behalf of her martyred husband's fame and her own welfare. Now sixty-six years of age, she was guest of honor at a reception in Chicago to raise money for a monument to the hero. It was a failure. She left with very little for herself. In Boston she made a better showing all around. At first the guest of the Sanborn family in Concord, she was then accorded a fine reception by the abolitionist remnant in Boston. A reporter found her dressed in black with white lace, a shawl draped over her shoulders. Her gray hair was combed straight back; her strong face was engraved with lines of grief; she held a bunch of tea roses in her hands. A second reception was sponsored by the New England Women's Club; and yet another was under black auspices. The funds sought in Boston were to be disbursed for the benefit of the family.[29] Mrs. Brown stopped at Topeka on the way home and was received in the Capitol by a large audience, including many blacks. She had already made a gift of family papers to the Kansas State Historical Society. At some later time the family would deposit the gold medal with that institution loyal to John Brown's memory.

Mrs. Brown's journey had taken on new significance when she learned in Chicago that the body of her son Watson, killed at Harpers Ferry bearing a flag of truce, had been recovered and would be placed at her disposal by a physician in Indiana who had come into possession of it. For years the cadaver had been on exhibit at the Winchester Medical College, in Virginia, and seekers after relics had carried off fingers, toes, and other parts. After her stepson John identified the body, it was bundled up and taken by Mrs. Brown for appropriate burial at North Elba.[30]

The four-room farmhouse at North Elba was scarcely imposing. As more than one traveler remarked, however, "The scenery is the grandest in the Adirondacks."[31] The unpromising farm lay in an upland valley densely wooded all about, but opening beautifully to Whiteface Mountain, 4,000 feet high. Three miles from Lake Placid, it was the only place of historical interest in this part of the Adirondacks. A good road now gave easy access, and with more and more summer colonists within reach, the place began to attract visitors. The property had passed to another family by 1870, when Kate Field, a capricious author, raised $2,000 to save it with the graveyard and 244 acres. The deed was in the name of the John Brown Association. It aimed at preservation, of course, but also at raising an appropriate monument on the property. Some years later, Kate Field also saved from destruction "John Brown's Fort," the Engine House, which, with other relics, had been exhibited at the Chicago World's Fair in 1893. Reassembled and restored, brick by brick, it remains today "the single most historic structure in Harper's Ferry National Park."[32]

A sojourner at John Brown's grave in 1865 wrote, "A finer spot for the tomb of a pious and brave man could not have been selected; and I could not help feeling how much the martyr must have gained in strength from his very residence. 'I lift up mine eyes upon the hills whence cometh my strength.'"[33] The body of John Brown lies between a huge granite rock chiseled with his name and the tombstone brought from his grandfather's grave in Torrington, Connecticut. The piety and simplicity of the place, some thought, was in perfect keeping with the man.

In 1896 the North Elba farm was conveyed to the state of New York as a park and a memorial to John Brown. Fifteen hundred people attended its dedication. No one, it seems, protested the raising of the state and the United States flags over the grave of the con-

John Brown's grave, photograph by S. R. Stoddard, ca. 1896
Library of Congress

victed traitor. A ten-foot monument, gift of the Memorial Association, was unveiled some distance away. President William McKin-
ley, the last of the presidents who fought in the Civil War, soon came
to pay his respects.

Three years later the bodies of seven of John Brown's men were
exhumed from a shallow unmarked grave on the banks of the Shenandoah River. They had been lost to memory as well as to sight for
forty-four years when Dr. Thomas Featherstonhaugh, medical ref-
eree at the Pension Bureau in Washington, after prolonged search,
located an elderly white man, James Foreman, who had helped to
bury the dead men and showed the doctor the exact site on the river.
Featherstonhaugh was acquainted with some members of the Brown
family and before his death donated his collection of books and photographs to the Library of Congress. He had thought, upon finding
the decomposed bodies, to inter them in the Engine House, once it
returned to Harpers Ferry, but dropped that idea when North Elba
became a state park.[34] Two other bodies, those of Aaron Stevens and

Albert Hazlett, had reposed all those years in friendly ground, in New Jersey. Sent forward from Perth Amboy, the remains of these comrades would rejoin those from the Shenandoah. Happily, the Reverend Joshua Young, who had officiated at the burial of the captain, was present on this occasion. It was an important milestone in the history of the legend. The work of the John Brown Association at North Elba was now virtually complete; and it turned attention to raising funds to acquire the original homestead in Torrington, Connecticut.

• • THE TRAIL of remembrance ran from Massachusetts to Kansas. Henry Andrew Wright, in the *New England Magazine,* identified the places where John Brown and his family had lived in Springfield, Massachusetts. There Douglass had come to meet him, and he had trumpeted the League of Gileadites. Brown was apparently well remembered in Springfield, though business misfortunes had cut short his stay.[35]

Although John Brown lived most of his life in Ohio, his time there was divided by a residence of ten years, 1825–35, in northwestern Pennsylvania. The path of settlement westward seems to have swept right by the village of Richmond, Crawford County, where Brown cleared five acres of virgin timber to build a tannery. Here his first wife, Dianthe Lusk, died, and he married Mary Anne Day, the daughter of a blacksmith in the neighborhood. Here he left the Masonic order, to which he had belonged briefly, after the notorious exposé in the aftermath of the mysterious disappearance of William Morgan in upstate New York. In Richmond, John Brown became a first citizen of the county. He started a church, built a schoolhouse, brought in the first blooded livestock, and helped to obtain a post office for the town, indeed was appointed the first postmaster by President John Quincy Adams. A leading resident of a later day remembered Brown from his boyhood. Always eager for mental and social improvement, he would gather his family, the tannery workers, and friends around a blazing fire and pose some great question, secular or religious, for discussion and debate. Brown, the leader, always had a decided opinion, it seems. Just why he chose to return to Ohio, or for that matter, why he had left it, is unclear; but it seems likely the tannery was a losing proposition in this backwater. There was a time after World War I when public-spirited citizens of New Richmond awoke to the memory of John Brown in their community. A memorial association was formed; a wall of the old tannery building was preserved; a highway marker was dedicated; and annual picnics in his honor were spread in the "Old Brown Grove." Yet not even the *W.P.A. Guide to the Keystone State* made mention of John Brown's decade-long residence there.[36]

John Brown was five years old when his father, Owen, brought his young family to Connecticut's Western Reserve in the new state of Ohio. An orthodox Congregationalist and an abolitionist, he passed his principles on to his first son. Settling in the brand-new town of Hudson, the Browns became part of the western phalanx of abolitionism out of New England. Always restless, ambitious for success, Brown, as he matured, tried his hand at many callings: shepherd, tanner, surveyor, land developer, wool trader. In 1823, when he had two children, he built a house adjoining his tannery in Hudson. The core of the house survives today. When he returned from Pennsylvania, Brown settled in a town not far from Hudson, Franklin Mills (now Kent), and plunged into a real estate scheme that looked promising because the projected Pennsylvania and Ohio Canal would go right by it. But the Panic of 1837 spoiled that scheme and Brown fell into bankruptcy. In 1849 he went out to the Alleghenies of Virginia to survey some of the 21,000 acres that Gerrit Smith, the abolitionist and philanthropist, had deeded to Oberlin College, partly with a view to acquiring land and resettling there; but the deal fell through. Fourteen of Brown's children were born in Ohio; some were buried there. In Richfield, another Western Reserve town where the family lived for a time, a cemetery plot holds four of John and Mary's children, Charles, Austin, Peter, and Sarah, at least three of whom died of the same affliction, probably dysentery, within days

of each other. On the burial stone is a crudely carved verse sometimes attributed to the children's father:

Through all the dreary night of death,
In fearful slumbers may you rest,
And when eternal day shall dawn,
And shades of death have passed and gone,
Oh, may you then, with a glad surprise,
In God's own image, wake and rise.[37]

If this was standard mortuary verse, the sentiments were surely
Brown's own.

Brown rebounded from business failure in 1844 when he entered
into partnership with Samuel Perkins Jr., a prosperous Akron wool
merchant. Presently Brown removed to Akron, where he is remembered today by not one but two monuments. The ever-resourceful
pioneer had a keen knowledge of sheep raising and wool grading. He
was a frequent contributor to the *Ohio Cultivator* and annually
walked off with prizes for the best sheep and finest wool. The company's flock was worth $20,000 in 1846 when Brown proposed that
the growers install an agent in New England to whom they could
ship their wool to be sorted and graded and, it was expected, sold at
a better price. Brown agreed to set up the agency in Springfield.
Things went well at first; then came the Walker Tariff, which de-
pressed prices for American wool. In 1849 Brown traveled to England with a large shipment of wool in hopes of finding a better mar-
ket abroad. Instead, according to the report of an American trader,
he met with disaster. Not only did he have to dispose of his wool at
half its value, but upon his return he found that the same stock had
been reshipped to Boston and sold with profit at a lower price than
prevailed when he left Springfield. The trader, Aaron Erickson,
wrote graphically of this business in a letter to Governor Wise in
1859. He concluded pointedly: "If I were in your powerful position, I
would no more permit this John Brown to be hanged than any other
lunatic in or out of an insane asylum."[38] This judgment seemed

Commemorative
stone and bronze
marker, Hudson,
Ohio
Photograph by author

harsh, as if business failure were a mark of lunacy. Apologists, finding nothing dishonest in Brown's conduct, tended to think him the
victim of circumstances he had neither the wit nor the dexterity to
overcome. Before the Panic of 1837 Brown was on the fast track to
commercial success. He was a bank director and the owner of many
thousands of dollars' worth of Ohio farmland. But his fortune col-
lapsed, as his oldest son explained, "and buried the reputation he had
achieved of possessing at least good common sense . . . in business
matters."[39] In retrospect, even his partner, Perkins, expressed disappointment in him.

It was in the Western Reserve of Ohio, more particularly in "the

John Brown tract," as it is sometimes known, from Ashtabula to Oberlin, that the struggling businessman made the resolute decision to devote his life to the destruction of slavery. Several of his children fixed the date in 1839, when he swore his whole family to the cause. The eldest, however, put the critical decision two years earlier, upon the death of the first abolitionist martyr, Elijah P. Lovejoy, of Illinois. In Hudson, remembered in history as "a rabid abolition town," a meeting was called at the Congregational Church to denounce the atrocity. Among the speakers was Owen Brown, fighting his habitual stammer. As the meeting drew to a close, his son John arose from a back bench, according to common report, raised his right hand, and declared, "Here, before God, in the presence of these witnesses, from this time, I consecrate my life to the destruction of slavery."[40] The children recalled as well their father's protest against racial segregation in the church they regularly attended in Franklin at that time. A group of blacks, some of them fugitives, had been seated near the back door behind the stove. Troubled by this segregation, Brown called it to the attention of the congregation: God was not "a respecter of persons," he said, and he invited the blacks to occupy his pew. "This was a bomb-shell," John Brown Jr. remembered.[41]

Wherever he lived, Brown was a helpmate to fugitive slaves. In Ohio there was a steady traffic between the river and the lakes, and Brown lent his hand to the Underground Railroad. One who knew him then, interviewed in 1879, said he was eccentric but not crazy, and as brave a man as ever drew breath. "I've seen him come in at night with [a] gang of five or six blacks that he had piloted all the way from the river, hide them away in the stables maybe, or the garret, and if anybody was following he would keep them stowed away for weeks."[42]

There is a rich trove of recollection of John Brown in Ohio. An Akron attorney, Daniel B. Hodley, who had known him when he was still in partnership with Perkins, was surprised to see the stranger in his office in August 1855. Waving a letter received from his beleaguered sons in Kansas, he said that despite his peaceable principles, he intended to go to their defense. At North Elba, with his wife, he had turned to the New Testament for guidance. Finding none, he turned to the Old Testament, where he read, "And the Lord said to Saul, Go out and slay the Philistines." He and Mary had then knelt in prayer and heard the Lord's voice: "John Brown, go to Kansas and slay the Border Ruffians!" Hearing Brown's account of this experience, Hodley agreed to call a meeting where Brown could speak and plead for guns and money to save Kansas from slavery.[43]

In his comings and goings to and from Kansas, the young state of Iowa figured prominently in John Brown's life. Tabor, in the southwest corner, had been founded in 1852 by a few families from Oberlin, most of them Congregationalists. When passage to Kansas by way of the Missouri River was blocked, an alternate land passage opened from Tabor to Nebraska City and south to the border. The town was also a station on the Underground Railroad. Brown first stopped there in September 1855. Two years later Hugh Forbes trained Brown's recruits in regular and irregular warfare at Tabor. Iowa furnished more men for the Harpers Ferry raid than any other state. At Springdale, a thriving Quaker settlement not far from Davenport, he enlisted the brothers Coppoc. Of course, nonviolence was a sacred vow of the Quakers. However, as Irving B. Richman wrote in 1894 of Brown and his followers, "much was pardoned to them by the Quakers because of the holiness of their object; for while the Quaker would not concede that bloodshed was ever right, it was with extreme leniency that he chided him who had shed blood to liberate the slaves."[44]

On his last visit to Tabor, Brown had eleven freed slaves from the notorious Missouri border raid in tow. The schoolhouse was placed at their disposal. The Sabbath was at hand, and Brown asked the minister, the Reverend John Todd, to proclaim a day of thanksgiving on behalf of himself, his comrades, and the freedmen. When the request was read from the pulpit, a stranger protested. Brown sought his withdrawal, but after a member objected, Brown himself withdrew. The Missouri foray and the reported price on the captain's head caused alarm among some of the citizens without really changing Tabor's opinion of John Brown. In any event, he met with a warmer welcome at Springdale, thanks mainly to Senator Josiah B. Grinnell. "Whole party and teams kept for Two days free of cost," the old warrior wrote of the reception; and "Last but not least Public thanksgiving to Almighty God offered up by Mr. Grinnell."[45]

To a handful of his Iowa friends Brown had confided his plan to attack slavery below the Potomac. One of these friends was Dr. George B. Gill, who later wrote that he had tried to persuade the captain of the folly of the scheme. "You and your handful of men cannot cope with the whole South," he said. Brown coolly replied, "I tell you, doctor, it will be the beginning of the end of slavery."[46] Both would be proved right. In August 1859 several men who had gotten wind of the plan conferred and prayed together at Springdale. It was agreed that something must be done to save the lives of the men embarked in the enterprise. Captain Brown was beyond persuasion; his young followers had implicit faith in him and were imbued with the spirit of martyrdom. The group adopted a scheme to send two anonymous letters of warning, one from Iowa, the other from Philadelphia, to John B. Floyd, secretary of war. One of the letters was received, but the secretary dismissed the information as incredible. After the event, the warning letter was released to the press. Its author, David J. Gue, was not identified until 1897.[47]

3

The Kansas Imbroglio

AT Osawatomie, Kansas, August 30, 1877, 10,000 people attended ceremonies to dedicate the monument to the fallen in the Battle of Osawatomie, more particularly to its hero, John Brown. Senator John J. Ingalls, orator of the day, declared the battle "our Thermopylae, John Brown our Leonidas." Charles Robinson, the first governor of the state after its admission to the Union in 1861, paid tribute to the embattled Free State settlers. And he lauded their revolutionary leader.

> The soul of John Brown was the inspiration of the Union armies in the emancipation war, and it will be the inspiration of all men in the present and distant future who may revolt against tyranny and oppression. . . . To the superficial observer John Brown was a failure. So was Jesus of Nazareth. Both suffered ignominious death as traitors to the government, yet one is now hailed as the Savior of the world from sin, and the other of a race from bondage.[1]

A few years later, Robinson would deeply regret those words, thinking them not only wrong but blasphemous. It was in Kansas, where John Brown's fame was born, that it would first be besmirched and befouled, and Robinson led the band of revilers.

The John Brown legend was inextricably bound up with what the Kansas historian James C. Malin later called "the legend of fifty-six." It was born in the toil and struggle of Bleeding Kansas, when virtual civil war raged between pro-slavery and antislavery forces to control the destiny of the territory. In the bitterness and acrimony of that conflict it was often difficult to distinguish between hero and villain, truth from propaganda; and the feelings thus generated carried over to the historic memory of persons and events. There were three main charges in the antihero image of John Brown in Kansas history: First, that although paraded as an important figure, indeed perhaps the most important, he was actually "a parenthesis in the history of Kansas."[2] Second, that at Pottawatomie Creek he committed the heinous crime of murdering or ordering the murder of five settlers. Third, that thereafter he was a negative influence in Kansas affairs, since his only goal was to make so much trouble as to incite a war, rather than to achieve order and reconciliation.

There were, of course, rear-guard defenders of Brown's role. Franklin Sanborn, in the wake of James Redpath, faithfully carried the torch for John Brown. So did William A. Phillips, an English immigrant who had gone to Kansas as a reporter for the *New-York Tribune* and in 1856 wrote *The Conquest of Kansas by Missouri and Her Allies*. Not only a reporter but in due course a soldier, congressman, and author, Phillips had an important place in the history of his adopted state. He admired Brown, with whom he had often talked, and never changed his opinion. "He sails with letters of marque from God," Phillips nimbly observed. In an article in the *Atlantic Monthly* in 1879, he recapitulated three interviews with Brown. At first Phillips found him something of an enigma, a compound of enthusiasm and cold intensity: "a volcano beneath a mountain of snow." In the second interview, Brown expressed fears that Robinson and his allies in the Free State Party would compromise with the enemy. Finally, on Brown's last visit to Kansas, in 1858, he appeared a virtual Spartacus, eager for war. Sitting in a small hotel room in Lawrence, Brown reviewed the history of slavery in America, concluding, "And now we have reached a point where nothing but war can settle the question." If the South were not checked in Kansas, he said, its advance would sound "the death-knell of republicanism" in the nation. But now he foresaw the victory of the new Republican Party in 1860 and, as in Spartacus's time, a war of slaves against masters. When Phillips expressed fear of such an outcome, Brown replied, "The world is too pleasant for you. But when your household gods are broken, as mine have been, you will see all this more clearly." They embraced and parted friends.[3]

Three years before his death in 1893, Phillips delivered a lecture before the Kansas State Historical Society in which he summed up his estimate of the martyred warrior:

> John Brown was more than a Kansas man. As a Kansas man he differed from some other Free State men; for while they passed resolutions, he acted [on] them. In his humble way he endeavored to pattern [himself] after the man of Galilee, and the part of the evangelists that seemed to impress him most was the occasion of our savior with whip of cords [driving] the money changers from the temple.

Closing, Phillips said Kansans should thank God for John Brown.[4]

Opinions were changing, however. Exhibit A in the Kansas case against John Brown was the Pottawatomie Massacre of May 23, 1856. It had been reported in the East, a congressional committee had been cognizant of it, yet little was known of the event publicly at the time of Harpers Ferry, and for years afterward Brown's complicity in it remained clouded. James Redpath said he had nothing to do with it. A credible eyewitness at last came forward in 1879. This was James Townsley of Osawatomie. His memory was impressively full and exact, so much so that it went virtually unchallenged. The *Lawrence Daily Journal,* on publishing Townsley's statement, called it "the most important contribution ever made to Kansas history."[5] The sixty-four-year-old man told how he had joined the Pottawatomie Rifle Company captained by John Brown Jr., in May, when the company marched for Lawrence, but turned back upon learning that the town had already been sacked by the Border Ruffians. He then fell in with a party of eight that included the elder Brown, four of his sons, and his son-in-law, armed with swords and pistols, who were drifting back home and looking for something outrageous to do. Getting word of the savage beating of Senator Charles Sumner of Massachusetts in the Capitol by a chivalrous South Carolinian only added to the men's frustration. Finally they came to the cabin of the Doyle family, known to be pro-slavery southerners. "The old man Doyle and two sons were called out and marched some distance from the house toward Dutch Henry's [Crossing] in the road, where a halt was made. Old John Brown drew his revolver and shot old man Doyle in the forehead, and Brown's two youngest sons immediately fell upon the younger Doyles with their two-edged swords." As the party proceeded, they slew two other settlers identified with the pro-slavery government. The ill-fated Doyles, according to a statement later attributed to the surviving widow, were inoffensive bystanders. Townsley said he had taken no part in the killings, indeed had made known his disapproval of them. But Brown told him they were necessary for the protection of free-state settlers, "that the pro-slavery party must be terrified" if freedom was to prevail. And as terrible as the transaction was, Townsley wrote, "I became satisfied that it resulted in good to the Free State cause." Redpath had taken an exculpatory view of the affair, and later hagiographers, such as Sanborn, while conceding that Brown ordered the murders, denied that he had pulled a trigger or wielded a sword. The only seriously disputed point in Townsley's report was that the old man shot and killed the elder Doyle. Salmon Brown, in his recollection of the atrocity, said, "Father never raised a hand in slaying the men. He shot a bullet into the head of old man Doyle about a half hour after he was dead, but what for I do not know."[6]

Long-time champions of John Brown and his place in Kansas history, such men as James Hanway, pleaded nolo contendere to Townsley's incrimination, though they might, as Hanway did, still believe that the effects of the killings and the terror were salutary. Charles Robinson, for his part, finally concluded that the effect was to unleash a wave of retaliation by the pro-slavery forces, renewing the conflict that Robinson and his moderate allies had virtually brought to a close. He laid out his case in a self-serving memoir, *The Kansas Conflict*, in 1892. Agent of the New England Emigrant Aid Company and leader of the Free State cause, Robinson admitted to having been deceived and misled about John Brown; now, some twenty years later, the Pottawatomie Massacre offered the key to unlock the Kansas struggle. Instead of retaliatory justification, it reignited the fuse of conflict. Robinson quoted Governor John Geary's impressions when he took up his duties in September 1856. "Desolation and ruin reigned on every hand; homes and firesides were deserted; the smoke of burning dwellings darkened the atmosphere; women and children, driven from habitations, wandered over the prairies and among the woodlands, or sought refuge and protection even among Indian tribes." This, Robinson maintained, was the work of John Brown. He sought war and revolution, first in Kansas, then in the nation. The battles that he advertised as his glory—Black Jack, Osawatomie, and the others—were all the result of the infamous massacre at Pottawatomie Creek. In "John Brown's Parallels," a composition much admired by his friends, he contrasted the Marais des Cygnes massacre by the Slave State captain, C. A. Hamilton, unnoticed and unpunished by any authority, with his own redemption from captivity of eleven Missouri slaves in 1858, which set federal marshals on his trail. "Eleven persons are peaceably restored to their natural and inalienable rights, with but one man killed, and 'all hell is stirred from beneath.'" Robinson maintained, however, that the true parallel to Hamilton's atrocity was the Pottawatomie Massacre. In his eyes Brown was a liar, a coward, a thief, and a murderer. His family was no better. Robinson closed his book on this note: "If history furnishes a parallel to the cold-blooded, unblinking persistence, and unscrupulous lying of John Brown, and his family, and friends, I have not discovered it; yet it is of such men some people make heroes." [7]

Robinson's change of mind on his old ally dismayed many Kansans. Some wondered if his spunky wife, Sara, a Kansas author in her own right, was not behind it. At any rate, he figured as the chief assassin in the John Brown legend. An old coadjutor from the Bleeding Kansas era, Dr. George W. Brown, publisher of the *Herald of Freedom* in beleaguered Lawrence, who might have laid claim to being the first anti-Brownist, for he had smashed the idol before there was a gallows, returned to the fray with *The Truth at Last.* Brown the journalist had removed to Rockford, Illinois, where the book ran serially in the local press before it was picked up in Kansas. Goaded by Robinson and Eli Thayer, father of the emigrant aid movement in the territory, Brown turned the old hero into the villain he had long suspected him to be. His policy was one of blood, the polemicist maintained; and the true heroes were men like Robinson and Thayer.[8]

The Kansas imbroglio soon spilled into the national press. In 1883 David N. Utter, a Unitarian minister in Chicago, wrote critically of the opinion of John Brown entertained in the eastern headquarters of the American Unitarian Association. "The Boston view of this old man and his deeds and motives needs correction by facts from Kansas which will some day cause men to cease paying tributes to his name."[9] An article from Utter's pen appeared in the *North American Review.* History had been extraordinarily kind to Brown, he wrote, largely because of lawless New England Transcendentalism. A new generation sought revaluation of the old hero. "The Zeitgeist has now more to say of science and fact than of right or value." Increasingly, as currents of doubt spread eastward, it was becoming a question whether John Brown deserved any eulogy whatsoever. Small errors in Utter's account of the Pottawatomie Massacre may be forgiven, but his interpretation of its effect on Brown was not only wrong but hysterical: "He could not live in Kansas, he could not live safely or peaceably anywhere. . . . The Rubicon had been passed. He cut off his long beard, probably in disguise and sought help in New England." (In fact, Brown twice returned to Kansas and only on the last tour did he have a beard.) "From that moment," Utter continued, "his whole object was to provoke the South to war." He was un-American and un-Christian. "His principles were those of the Russian nihilists."

Utter was answered by Senator John Ingalls, a Kansas Republican weaned on the John Brown legend. Thinking the article puerile, he deigned to answer it. Closing, he called up all of Brown's battles, from Franklin to Sugar Creek, Black Jack, and Osawatomie, and said that after this no hateful slights or falsehoods could perturb his soul. There were also replies to the cleric from John Brown Jr. in the *Cleveland Leader*, Richard Hinton in the *Chicago Times*, and Sanborn in the *Springfield Republican*. The meeting rooms of the Massachusetts Historical Society were ruffled by ill-tempered remarks on the old hero by Amos Lawrence, who had supplied him with arms and money in the Kansas conflict. He had, it seemed, been deceived by John Brown, now revealed as "an unprincipled ruffian." James Freeman Clarke, the soul of Boston Unitarianism, replied to Lawrence at the next meeting of the society. He lauded John Brown as a Puritan of the Cromwell type; and when the law of God and the law of man came into conflict, he dutifully chose the former.[10]

For several years Eli Thayer, founding director of the New England Emigrant Aid Company, had been panting for a share of the glory of the Kansas crusade. To embellish his own reputation he seemed to think it necessary to tear down John Brown's. At any rate, he thought that the contribution of his organization to Kansas had been neglected. Former abolitionists denied the premise. The Emigrant Aid Company cared more about profits from real estate than about freedom in Kansas, they thought. Thomas Wentworth Higginson, writing in the *Boston Daily Advertiser*, said that the movement to organize emigrant communities was a failure. "What the society really did was to advertise Kansas."[11] His opinion was subsequently corroborated by John G. Nicolay and John Hay, biographers of Abraham Lincoln. Thayer persevered with his campaign in the press and finally, in 1889, published his *History of the Kansas Crusade*. The victory belonged to peaceable aid societies such as his, the book claimed, not to John Brown and the Garrisonians, who wanted disunion and war. Nicolay and Hay, by the way, wrote a belittling chapter on Brown, quite in keeping with the reproachful view of him that came out of Kansas.[12]

•• FRANKLIN B. Sanborn's long-awaited *Life and Letters of John Brown* made its appearance in the thick of the Kansas controversy in 1885. The author was then fifty-four years old. He had devoted half his life to his hero, first as friend and counselor, then as the self-appointed guardian of his reputation. Brown remained a theme of Sanborn's life for the thirty-two years that still lay before him, though it took second place to his literary career, chiefly as a memoirist of New England authors. Sanborn, it may be recalled, was a young Concord schoolmaster and abolitionist when he met Osawatomie Brown in 1857. He became one of the Secret Six who advised, armed, and bankrolled Brown, then watched over his fame after his death. Sanborn himself was no hero; he decamped twice to Canada to evade testimony on Harpers Ferry, and he did not choose to fight in the Civil War. Over the years he was particularly attentive to Brown's family—two daughters, Anne and Sarah, studied for a time in Sanborn's school—and he often contributed to the *Atlantic Monthly* and to leading newspapers—the *Springfield Republican*, the *Boston Transcript, New-York Tribune*—on Brown's behalf.

Sanborn's book was unabashedly a work of advocacy, but that is not to say it should be dismissed, as some critics were wont to do, as a mere apology for Brown. With Carlyle and Emerson and others of the time, Sanborn subscribed to the great-man theory of history.

> He [Brown] was one of ten thousand, and, as Thoreau said, could not be tried by a jury of his peers, because his peers did not exist; yet so much was he in accord with what is best in American character, that he will stand in history as one type of our people, as Franklin and Lincoln do—only with a difference. He embodied the distinctive qualities of the Puritan, but with a strong tincture of the humane sentiments of later times.[13]

As his greatness was given to the cause of human freedom, he found his place in the ongoing history of freedom in Western civilization.

The book was well named: *The Life and Letters of John Brown.* Perhaps one-half of the 300,000 or more words belonged to letters, recollections, and similar primary sources. Much of this material was new, such as Brown's unfinished essay of 1850, "Sambo's Mistakes," a work suggestive of Benjamin Franklin's *Poor Richard's Almanac,* in which, as Sanborn said, the author sought to bring black freedman "to a better knowledge of their position, and to form habits that would fit them for freedom."[14] Such materials added fresh and vivid touches to the characterization of the hero; and the author was not averse to trimming and straightening his prose. Sanborn's research was not that of a scientific historian or an exact editor, rather that of a nineteenth-century man of letters. Yet, taken on its own terms, the work was immensely valuable.

Only a descendant of the Puritans could have understood so well the power of religion in the hero's life. "The story of John Brown will mean little to those who do not believe that God governs the world," Sanborn wrote, "and that He makes His will known in advance to certain chosen men and women who perform it, consciously or unconsciously."[15] He went on to compare Brown with Cromwell and Milton. And he introduced a long letter of some 2,000 words that John Brown had written to his eldest son expounding his Calvinistic understanding of Scripture. In it the kingdom of God and the affairs of the world are one. The divine mission given to John Brown was to annihilate slavery. There were early portents, but the revelation came to him in a blaze of light in 1837. It was the first time, the younger John Brown said, he ever saw his father kneel in prayer; and he told all the older children of his purpose to make war on slavery and implored God's blessing on the undertaking. This episode coincided with the pledge at the Lovejoy meeting. But the question of just when and under what impulse John Brown vowed to destroy slavery was still in dispute. Wendell P. Garrison, for one, drawing upon memorandum books got from family members, argued that it came some years later.[16]

Sanborn had long denied Brown's participation in the Pottawatomie Massacre. Now, in the wake of James Townsley's testimony, he sought to mitigate and extenuate the crime. The real crime, of course, was committed by the national government, which had made Kansas a battleground. Such was the theme of Senator Charles Sumner's great speech that provoked the murderous assault upon him precisely one day before the massacre. That was a retaliatory blow, justified by its effects, widely acknowledged at the time; and it was destined to make Kansas free. "Such a deed," the author wrote, "must not be judged by the every-day rules of conduct, which distinctly forbid violence and the infliction of death for private causes." It was a public deed, comparable to the violent deeds of commanding generals in the Civil War. Admitting now that Brown was the *instrument* in the murders of the men at Pottawatomie Creek, Sanborn still denied that he had raised his own hand or discharged his own weapon. "He was no less responsible for their death than if he had done so, and this he never denied."[17]

For many years Sanborn and Robinson engaged in an angry quarrel over the retrospective judgment on the Pottawatomie Massacre and its significance for Brown's legacy. The governor's change of mind on the old hero was a public embarrassment. He did what he could to justify himself, blackening Brown's character at every turn. The captain's foray into Missouri to rescue slaves, for instance, was the work of a robber and an outlaw; after that incursion he went to Harpers Ferry and "displayed his wonderful generalship in committing suicide."[18] In 1885 Sanborn initiated a correspondence in the *Boston Transcript* on what he called "the Rescue of Kansas." The three rescuers were Robinson, Thayer, and George Washington Brown. Robinson, he insisted, had always known Brown was the author of the blow at Pottawatomie, indeed may have authorized it. Pleas of ignorance or innocence until Townsley's testimony would not do, nor would the plea that he, with so many others, had been deceived about Brown's character. Robinson's reply, earlier observed, was to brand Sanborn, together with Brown's family and such apologists as Hanway, liars.[19]

Sanborn's account of Brown's relationships with the Secret Six, from 1857 to 1859, was disappointing. Its sketchiness may be attributed, in part, to the fact that he destroyed possibly incriminating correspondence after the Harpers Ferry raid, as did several of his associates, though some letters survived. Having dodged testimony himself, Sanborn thereafter made no secret of his devotion to John Brown. It was, in fact, the boast of his life. He was disturbed, nevertheless, that some others of the martyr's confidants had remained in a state of denial. He turned the focus on Gerrit Smith, whom Brown had known the longest. In 1872 the *Atlantic Monthly* published an article, "John Brown and His Friends," without attribution of authorship, though knowledgeable persons readily inferred it was from Sanborn's pen. The material in this article was now woven into his biography of Brown.[20]

Sanborn told how in February 1858 he journeyed to Peterboro, New York, Smith's home, for an urgent meeting with the captain. He was returning, unhappily, to Kansas after Hugh Forbes's betrayal. To the Secret Six he had already hinted at the "Virginia plan." Now he offered more detail. To Sanborn alone, according to the author, he named the point of attack, Harpers Ferry. He showed both Gerrit Smith and Sanborn, as well as Edwin Morton, Smith's guest and a Harvard classmate of Sanborn, the constitution he had drafted for government of liberated territory in the mountains. "Without accepting Brown's plans as reasonable," Sanborn wrote, "we were prepared to second them merely because they were his—under the impulse of that sentiment which [Governor John] Andrew afterward gave utterance when he said: 'Whatever might be thought of John Brown's acts, John Brown himself was right.'" They talked at length over two days. Afterward Smith, sixty-one years of age, and Sanborn, twenty-six, agreed to stand by the old warrior all the way. The co-conspirators later ratified the pledge with dollars and rifles. Yet the shock of Harpers Ferry twenty months later sent Smith to an insane asylum and the others into various states of panic. Upon his release, Smith pleaded ignorance of Brown's invasion plan, and did so to the day of his death in 1874. Stearns and Howe had also claimed ignorance under oath before the Senate investigating committee, where the questions were so clumsily framed that they were able to evade the truth without "literal falsehood." Yet Sanborn was troubled for years by the question: How could these distinguished men deny knowledge of the Harpers Ferry attack simply because they did not know, or could not guess, that Brown meant to begin there? Finally, with regard to the magazine article, Sanborn asked Smith if he would object to publication of his prior knowledge of the plan first laid out in detail under his own roof. In reply, Smith begged to be spared any such revelation until after his death. Mrs. Smith, citing "painful sensations," added her own plea for silence.

In 1877, three years after Smith's death, Octavius Brooks Frothingham published his biography based on the personal papers. Smith's footprints were all over Harpers Ferry. He and Brown thought alike and had the same goals, though Brown was the more visionary and the more radical. Smith might have been tried and convicted of conspiracy against the United States, Frothingham wrote. At this revelation, Smith's daughter, who owned the plates of the book, stopped the presses after a thousand copies had been printed by G. P. Putnam. In the revised edition issued the following year, the implication that Smith knew more than he had admitted was missing.[21]

• • THE ATTACK on John Brown's character in history was offset, if not deflected, by several mitigating factors. One was, quite simply, continued fascination with the person of John Brown. While not readily associated with humor, he sometimes showed a playful and amusing side that softened the austere image. In 1881 Judge Thomas Russell, in whose home the Kansas fugitive had found shelter, made an address to the Massachusetts Club, in Boston, peppered with anecdotes about his notorious guest. Playing with the Russells' eighteen-month-old daughter, the old man remarked, "Now, when I am being hung for treason, you can say that you used to stand on old Captain Brown's hand." Lydia Maria Child, remembered for her poem on the blessed kiss, relished the story of a Missouri slaveholder who had gone to Osawatomie to claim a fugitive slave. After he recovered the slave, he encountered Brown and his men, who took off the master's hat and coat and put them on the slave. Having dismounted the master, they put the slave in the saddle and sent him off. "It took Kansas to turn the tables so handsomely as that," Mrs. Child wrote, and even the solemn captain must have laughed heartily. "Bravo for Kansas!"[22] To those who accused Brown of stealing horses, he dryly replied that he had only "liberated" them. The Kansas professor Leverett W. Spring, whose book on the Kansas troubles drew Sanborn's rebuke, showed the hero's lighter side in an article, "Catching Old John Brown," in *Overland Monthly.* Presumably truthful, it concerns the federal marshals' clumsy attempt to capture the prodigious fighter. One pair sent to arrest him are stripped of their clothes instead; and when a territorial judge appears to take him into custody, Brown turns the tables, declaring, "You are my prisoner." J. W. Winkley, in his *John Brown the Hero,* conjured up a cyclonic force, à la Mike Fink or Davey Crockett. To a squad of Border Ruffians, sent out to capture him but themselves made captive, Brown said forgivingly, "Go in peace. Go home and tell your neighbors and friends of your mistake. . . . Go home and become liberty-loving citizens." Such was his news for the Missourians.[23]

John Brown figured prominently in the periodical press of the late nineteenth century. Illustrated monthly magazines such as *Century, McClure's,* and *Outlook* often gave space to him in their pages; and *Peterson's Magazine* serialized a biography of him. His name often turned up in daily newspapers. St. Louis readers may have been surprised to find in the *Globe-Democrat,* April 8, 1888, Judge Richard Parker's first statement on John Brown's trial in almost thirty years.

He continued to believe he had presided in "a just and humane spirit." He scoffed at the idea of Brown's insanity, and gave his impressions of some of the other defendants. In retrospect, he observed that had Brown deferred his invasion for a week, he would not have been brought to trial until the succeeding May—such was the court's calendar—which raised an interesting hypothetical "if." Andrew Hunter, the prosecuting attorney, about the same time published his reflections on the raid. He spoke of efforts to recover John Brown's carpetbag, with incriminating letters, mysteriously lost, though it would finally be found.[24]

Without having made up their collective mind about John Brown, the American people remained interested in him. He was the great enigma of the Civil War era. Perhaps Albion Tourgee, the novelist, said it best:

> John Brown! Monster and Martyr; Conspirator and Saint; Murderer and Liberator; Cause and Consequence! Alerting one-half the land to emulate his example; stimulating the other to meet aggression; inciting both to shedding of blood! Brave, humble, simple-hearted, simple living. Seeking not his own gain. Cruel in the scathing intensity of his hate for wrong. Grand in the impossibility of his attempt. Sublime in his faith that through his death the purpose of his life would be performed. The climax of one age and the harbinger of another![25]

With respect to the Kansas image, it is impossible to overlook the work of the Kansas State Historical Society under a secretary, Franklin G. Adams, who relished John Brown's fame, and a train of successors of the same mind. Adams cultivated the interests of the Brown family and of such eastern advocates as Sanborn and Mrs. George L. Stearns, the widow whose adulation of John Brown surpassed even that of her late husband. Mary Brown's visit to Topeka in 1882, at the invitation of the society, sealed the family relationship; and its occurrence at the time of the furor over the Pottawatomie Massacre cushioned this blow to the legend. Her reception over five days, following upon a reunion of John Brown associates, was one long salute to the martyr. She was, after all, as she was hailed in the Capitol, "the widow of the man who did more than any other to render the name of Kansas immortal."[26]

Mrs. Stearns, in a letter addressed to Mrs. Brown on the first anniversary of Martyr's Day, 1860, said her husband had "ploughed up the public mind thoroughly, all over the country; and I have availed myself of the opportunity to throw in seed liberally." So she did. In 1878, after a prolonged illness, she wrote to Senator Ingalls proposing that the State of Kansas commission a statue of John Brown for the newly inaugurated Statuary Hall of the United States Capitol. Ingalls referred the letter to Franklin Adams. He not only applauded the idea but agreed with Mrs. Stearns that the Edwin Brackett bust (see p. 42), which she owned, should serve as the model. As the only life portrait of John Brown other than photographs, it was virtually indispensable. A copy of the bust was sent to Paris for the Exposition. The following year, 1879, a bill was introduced in the state legislature to fill the two Kansas positions in Statuary Hall with likenesses of John Brown and Jim Lane, his lesser-known Kansas ally. However, a committee reported adversely on the proposal, as Adams informed Mrs. Stearns, citing the unsettled state of opinion on the subject. G. W. Brown's book, followed by Utter's attack, disturbed Mary Stearns. Adams wrote to reassure her: "It has done no harm to the memory of John Brown." Her son, Frank Stearns, took up the cudgel, contributing "Justice for John Brown" to the *Boston Transcript*. As if to vindicate Adams's confidence, the *Topeka Daily Capital*, in 1897, conducted a contest on the two great Kansans to fill those places in the U.S. Capitol. To no one's surprise, John Brown headed the list. Alas, the honor would never be bestowed on him. (Kansas finally chose to be represented by Ingalls and a little-known governor.) Honors are chancy and infinitely varied, of course. Be it noted that in 1905 the U.S. battleship *Kansas* was christened with water drawn from the John Brown Spring near Osawatomie.[27]

Through Franklin Adams, Mrs. Stearns arranged to scatter busts of Brown across Kansas. While not without critics, the Brackett bust was much admired. Mrs. Brown had shed tears upon seeing it in Boston. In the obituary of Mary Stearns that Sanborn wrote for the Kansas State Historical Society, he recalled how the Brackett bust came into being. After her husband gave his support to the sculptor's project to go to Charles Town, Mrs. Stearns warned him to expect Brown's opposition. He would say, "Nonsense. Better give the money to the poor." At that point, she counseled, Brackett must say he had come at Mrs. Stearns's request. That was exactly Brown's response, Brackett reported upon his return, but then he consented, saying, "Anything Mr. and Mrs. Stearns desire. Take my measurements."[28]

Not all members of the Historical Society approved the portraits of Brown that filled the walls. The model photographic likeness, from 1859, is usually attributed to James Wallace Black, of Boston (see p. 10). It is three-quarters length and shows a benign and full-bearded head, slightly turned, and gazing intently into the camera. Brown printed the image on autograph cards to pass out to friends and acquaintances; and ovals of this portrait often turned up. The first fine oil painting of John Brown, by Nahum B. Onthank, was derived from this likeness. The photograph, however, may not have been taken by Black. J. B. Heywood, in a statement found in the Stearns Collection, in Topeka, says that *he* took the picture in the summer of 1859, at the instance of the New England Aid Society, in his studio at 173 Washington Street. "I disposed of my place of business afterwards," Heywood explained, "to J. W. Black." The negative went with the sale.[29]

• • RICHARD J. Hinton's *John Brown and His Men,* in 1894, was a valuable addition to the growing John Brown literature. Hinton, another Englishman by birth who found his way to Bleeding Kansas as a newspaper reporter, focused on the fighting men around the captain, not only those at Harpers Ferry but others in Kansas. He first met Brown at the Nebraska line in 1856. He remembered him then as a tall, sinewy figure with a long rugged face, keen eyes, a roman nose, and a firm chin; he had "the look of the uncowed man in constant danger and always on the watch."[30] This was the image of the Fighter. Another image, "the deeper ensemble," featuring the flowing beard, in 1859, was that of the Prophet. The men who followed John Brown were a remarkable galaxy. Ohio-born John Henri Kagi was also a newspaper correspondent drawn to Brown in Kansas. The ablest of Brown's followers, Kagi was second in command at Harpers Ferry, where he lost his life. Aaron Dwight Stevens hailed from Connecticut; his great-grandfather had fought in the American Revolution, his grandfather in the War of 1812, and he himself was a veteran of the Mexican War. He joined Brown in Kansas, was pitifully wounded at Harpers Ferry, and met his death on the same scaffold as the captain. John E. Cook, also from Connecticut, was wellborn and well educated. Attracted to the captain in Kansas, he was the first recruit for Harpers Ferry. Cook was the only captive to write a "confession." Although he made an escape, Cook was recaptured and hanged. It was fitting that Hinton, the memorialist of John Brown's men, was asked to deliver the address on the burial of the last of the fallen comrades at North Elba.

The American publication in 1889 of the English translation of Hermann von Holst's extended essay, *John Brown*, was made possible by Frank Stearns, to whom, when a lad, Brown had addressed the memoir of his childhood. Alarmed, like his mother, by recent attacks on the hero's fame in Kansas, Stearns had cast about for a brief biography truthful to the man and accessible to a wide audience. Holst's book, in German, came to his attention. Stearns arranged for its translation and publication. By this time the author had immigrated to the United States and presently became professor of history at the University of Chicago. His seven-volume *Constitutional and Political History of the United States* (1876–92) was written in the spirit of consummate nationalism. John C. Calhoun, with the southern slavocracy, was the villain of the work; John Brown, with Abraham Lincoln, stood at the head of the heroes. Brown, Holst wrote, "was a man of the old covenant," who added "a really remarkable talent for guerrilla warfare," and who in Kansas "startled the whole South like a bursting bombshell." Of the raid at Harpers Ferry he remarked, "The plan was so nonsensical that it was an unseemly piece of pleasantry on the part of the Attorney General to accuse Brown of high treason." In the end, Holst echoed Hugo: it was not Brown but slavery that hanged on the gallows.[31]

George W. Curtis, among the most prominent authors and orators of the late nineteenth century, delivered many times, before many audiences, an oration in which he contrasted the careers of Calhoun and Brown, "the two most illustrious fanatics in our history," one dying in his bed, the other on the gallows.

> The felon stoops beneath the gallows, and tenderly lifting a child of the degraded race, kisses her in the soft winter sun. Peace! Peace! History and the human heart will judge between them. Both their bodies lie mouldering in the grave; whose soul is marching on? It was the fanaticism of abolitionism that has saved this country from the fanaticism of slavery. It's fire fighting fire. And the fire of Heaven is prevailing over that of Hell.[32]

Poets continued to be attracted to John Brown. The most ambitious of the poems in this period was "John Brown and the Heroes of Harpers Ferry," by William E. Channing, the Concord friend of Sanborn. Essentially a rhymed narrative, it gave out a wooden peal. More engaging were verses that had a certain moral resonance. The best of them, titled simply "John Brown," was by a little-known poet, William Herbert Carruth:

> Had he been made of such poor clay as we—
>   Who when we feel a little fire aglow
>   'Gainst wrong within us, dare not let it grow.
> But crouch and hide it, lest the scorner see

And sneer, yet bask our self-complacency
   In that faint warmth,—and had it been fashioned so
   The Nation ne'er had come to that birth-throe
That gave the world a new Humanity.

He was no mere professor of the word—
   His life a mockery of his creed;—he made
No discount on the Golden Rule, but heard
   Above the senate's brawls and din of trade
Ever the clank of chains, until he stirred
The nation's heart by that immortal raid.[33]

One of the John Brown Kansas loyalists, William Elsey Connelly, published a biography of the old hero in Topeka in 1900. (He and Hinton also embarked on an abortive project to collect and publish Brown's writings.) An epigraph taken from the Kansas "poet laureate," Eugene Ware, who wrote as Ironquill, abridged the author's message:

John Brown of Kansas:
   He dared to begin;
     He lost
   But, losing, won.[34]

History, that is to say the Civil War, had proved John Brown right, and before that overwhelming truth, personal failures and crimes faded into insignificance. Connelly got most of his data from Sanborn and Hinton and from Daniel W. Wilder's *Annals of Kansas;* but he had his own story to tell of the Pottawatomie Massacre. Here he emphasized the provocation: the sacking of Lawrence, the atrocities committed in the retreat of the invaders to Missouri, and the real danger that the pro-slavery settlers at Dutch Henry's Crossing would attack the Browns and their allies. "They had whetted a sword for the Free-State settlers."[35] It was, in sum, self-defense.

In Kansas, at least, the John Brown legend was guarded from attack because it was inseparable from the legend of the state. "To be a Son or Daughter of the Revolution or a member of the Cincinnati," it was said in an eastern journal, "is as nothing compared to the fortune of having been a Free State fighter."[36] The generation that followed the war was the fertile time for recollections and memoirs. And to defame John Brown was a little like defaming Kansas history. During these years, too, the state was acquiring a substantial minority of black citizens. They had been unknown and unwanted during the state's troubled birth, much to Captain Brown's disgust. But with the collapse of Reconstruction and the rise of Jim Crow in the southern states, Kansas was flooded with black refugees. As many as 500 a month came, some 20,000 altogether. "Go west, young black man," wrote a St. Louis newspaper editor. "Go west to Kansas, where John Brown's soul is doing perpetual guard duty." Brown having been the hero of abolition in Kansas, many blacks, it seemed, looked upon the state as the land of Canaan. They were called "Exodusters."[37]

William Allen White, among the best-known Kansans of the new century, saw that the earlier reaction against John Brown was a passing phase, and that his soul would indeed go marching on. In an astute estimate of the man and the legend he wrote:

> He was in the unfettered language of the bounding West what we would call a hell-raiser. His life settled no controversy; his deeds accomplished no great results; but, nevertheless, he was needed, and without him the abolition of human slavery might have been postponed for many years. Every great movement needs an agitator. Every leader of spiritual ideals needs a John the Baptist.

White, a reform-minded Republican, thought that the Progressivism of the new century rang with the spirit and agitation of John Brown. "We are going through the *John Brown cycle* today." White trusted that the Lincoln cycle would follow.[38]

On the fiftieth anniversary of Bleeding Kansas, 1906, whence the John Brown legend took its rise, the *New-York Tribune* published an essay by Sanborn and an editorial, "Osawatomie Brown." Sanborn followed Emerson in ranking the hero's speech to the court at Charles Town with Lincoln's Gettysburg Address, and forecast that Brown would in time become a mythical figure like King Arthur and Joan of Arc. The editorial noted the wide difference of opinion on Brown, either saint or devil, hero or traitor, and observed that though the great issues of his day were gone, they would continue to appear under new guise. For instance, "There are those who see in every denial of the right of freedom of labor under whatever compulsion, and in every discrimination between men on purely racial grounds, whether in New England or South Carolina, an indication of the need that John Brown's soul shall still be marching on."[39] This assessment echoed that of the Kansas editor.

4

The Great Biography

A T   T H E turn of the twentieth century, one hundred years after
John Brown's birth—an anniversary virtually unnoticed publicly—his place in American memory, along with the staying power
of the legend gathered round him, was uncertain. His reputation had
been shaken by the revelations in Kansas, where it was born; and as
the passions generated by the Civil War cooled, the pillar of the legend, the martyrdom at Harpers Ferry, seemed likely to tremble.

John Brown was, in some sense, an anachronism when he appeared on the stage of history. "Brown, in truth," Charles Eliot Norton wrote, "was a man born out of time. . . . He belonged to the
Covenanters, with the Puritans. He was possessed of an idea which
mastered his whole nature and gave dignity and force to his character."[1] Man and idea proved immensely valuable. All honor was due
John Brown. Yet, throwback that he was, how likely was it that his
fame would echo down the corridors of time? How could his sacrifice
inspire generations to come? How could his biblicism be transliter-
ated into the language of an increasingly secular age? What light did
his life cast upon the changing problems of modern America?

In Thomas Carlyle's typology of the hero—divinity, prophet,
poet, priest, king, man of letters—Brown fitted most closely the
priest, or spiritual captain. "Is not every true reformer by the nature
of him, a Priest first of all?" the English author asked.[2] If so, the

American was in danger of being buried, like Cromwell, under the odium that posterity heaped upon unbridled fanatics.

Regardless, the martyred hero had several things going for him. First, he was on the right side of history. He was an authentic American revolutionary, in the grain of freedom and equality. Second, he was a lightning rod of controversy, saint to some, devil to others, and fame is nourished by argument, whatever the outcome. Third, if Brown conveyed to posterity no developed doctrine or ideology, he was still a powerful symbol. In short, his soul went marching on, and it could be invoked in any crisis that had the color of freedom fighting oppression.

American historians, in their accounts of the war era, offered a gauge of the fame posterity would assign to John Brown. None doubted that he played a significant part in the coming of the war, whether or not he was necessary to it. The historians made strikingly different estimates of Brown as a man and a leader. Allusion was earlier made to Holst's compendious history; it was the work most partial to Brown. (Curiously, Holst was the only historian with professional credentials to essay a biography of John Brown.) A Confederate general turned historian, Marcus J. Wright, wrote a rebuttal to Holst's critical treatment of the trial at Charles Town. It was the accused alone who gave the trial dignity, the German thought. Wright lauded the judge and the prosecutor. National historians generally downplayed Brown's role in Kansas and focused instead on the raid at Harpers Ferry. Writing of that event, James Schouler, the Yankee author of a seven-volume *History of the United States,* turned his rebuke not on Brown and his deluded men but on the unreasoned and vengeful response of the captors, for it was they who made a small event into a great one. Brown was an enthusiast against slavery, the author said; he was not a felon.[3]

John W. Burgess, a university professor and the author of the authoritative *Civil War and the Constitution,* thought the villainy at Harpers Ferry worthy of "His Satanic Majesty himself." It solidified the planter leadership in the South, and for that reason, said Burgess, must be counted among the "chiefest crimes of our history." Albert Bushnell Hart, of Harvard, editor of the compendious New American Nation series, assigned the volume *Causes of the Civil War* to F. E. Chadwick, a naval officer by profession. Chadwick set out to correct what he considered "the extreme laudation of Brown" in historical literature, yet his harshest strictures were reserved for the captain's counselors, who lied and dissembled to create a cover for him. Hart was displeased by the volume. "If John Brown is to retain his position as a national hero he must be set forth by a sympathetic hand," the professor wrote to Oswald Garrison Villard, a former student about to undertake a full-scale biography of Brown.[4]

Woodrow Wilson, in his protracted *History of the American People,* called the raid at Harpers Ferry "sinister," at the same time conceding a certain grandeur to its leader. This was as far as a native southerner could go. Southern writers in general were unforgiving. The most popular Confederate history of the war—the textbook of schoolchildren—held that Brown invaded Virginia "to murder the white men, women and children." Southern accounts tended to run to defamation. Thus John A. Wyeth, a Confederate surgeon, said of Brown in his recollections: "Having failed at every one of a half-dozen different vocations to make a living for his family and himself, he was a rolling stone so mossless that at the age of fifty-five he was absolutely bankrupt in fortune, and no less so in honorable reputation." So he turned, embittered, to murder and treason in Kansas and Virginia.[5]

The most discerning discussion of John Brown by a major historian was that of James Ford Rhodes in his *History of the United States from the Compromise of 1850.* An Ohio-born Republican, Rhodes was wholeheartedly on the side of the Union and against slavery. He described the fifty-five-year-old abolitionist at his arrival in Kansas: a stern Calvinist, an ascetic in his habits, inflexible in his temper, upright in his intentions. At Pottawatomie he sought to expiate the blood of five free-state men with an equal number of pro-slavery victims. "What the world called murder was for him the decree of

God." Rhodes found no reason to believe the massacre aided the free-state cause. But Brown showed a talent for guerrilla warfare in Kansas, and it led him to Harpers Ferry. The long interview after his capture there and his conduct throughout the trial, wrote Rhodes, "revealed a heroic spirit with an ideal passing comprehension." Of course the attack was an act of folly, yet its captain was "as sane a man as ever lived."[6] In this judgment Rhodes was in accord with Schouler and Holst, as well as Edward Channing, the Harvard professor whose multivolume *History of the United States* appeared twenty-five years later. Channing was the first student to make a connection between Brown's early vocation as a shepherd and his zealotry against slavery. "Long vigil and hours of solitude had led him to that excessive contemplation which seems to be the breeding ground of fanaticism." With regard to his mental state, Channing continued, it should be remembered that the line between the sane and the insane is exceedingly difficult to draw. Besides, Thermopylae was as desperate a gamble as Harpers Ferry; and what of Captain John Parker at Lexington? Was he insane?[7] For Channing, Rhodes, and many others, the charge that Brown was mad or insane was simply an excuse to rob his life and death of dignity. Still, Brown *was* an enigma. "A century may, perchance, pass," Rhodes concluded his discussion, "before an historical estimate acceptable to all lovers of liberty can be made of John Brown."[8]

John Brown, meanwhile, was becoming a subject of historical fiction. Three novels published from 1895 to 1899 made him a central character. (Here the French were ahead of the Americans. *Un Drame Esclavagiste, or Prologue to the American Secession, with Notes on John Brown*, by H. E. Chevalier, appeared in 1878. In this romance, discovered at the Paris Exposition, Edwin Coppoc is the protagonist.) The first of the American works was *Katy of Catoctin*, by the irrepressible journalist George A. Townsend (Gath). Described as "a national romance," it is set in the highlands of the Catoctin valley, not far from Harpers Ferry, where the young hero encounters a stranger in the woods who calls himself Isaac Smith (Brown's alias in

Maryland). A topsy-turvy romance threads through the course of events, culminating in Harpers Ferry; the tale closes with Booth's assassination of Lincoln. Arthur Paterson's *For Freedom's Sake* was published in Philadelphia after running serially in the weekly edition of the *London Times.* Set in Kansas during its time of troubles, the book describes the romantic adventure of its Boston abolitionist hero and his southern-born golden-haired maiden. She sees John Brown as a warrior savior out of a novel by Sir Walter Scott; and he, indeed, becomes the couple's protector and deliverer.

The best of these novels was Elbert Hubbard's *Time and Chance.* Well known as the founder of the Roycroft artist colony in East Aurora, New York, Hubbard was fascinated by the character of John Brown. He owned a marble bust of the hero by Jerome Conner, and made a conjectural portrait of him at forty-two for the novel's frontispiece. The book is a historical romance, much in the vein of such best-selling authors as Mary Johnston and Winston Churchill at the turn of the century. John Brown is introduced as a twelve-year-old tagging after his father in aiding runaway slaves. Adventures with the Underground Railroad run through the book. John Brown devises a wagon with a false bottom and trapdoor, laughingly called "Brown's Patent Adjustable Nigger Carriage." A devoted partner in this work is a secret love, Margaret, in Kentucky. This is the first suggestion that Brown was any kind of gallant. He meets up with Captain Brydger, Margaret's son, in Kansas. After settling things there, Brown goes to her Kentucky mansion and together they plan the Harpers Ferry invasion. Mary Brown is never mentioned. The night before his execution, the martyr writes his last letter to Margaret. "I am happy, happier than ever before in my life. I die tomorrow and my only regret is that in this life I cannot repay you even in part for all you have done for me. Farewell!" Obviously, Hubbard strayed far from the historical record.[9] *Time and Chance* passed through several editions. One of its admiring readers was a West Virginia youth, Boyd Stutler, and it set him on a trail of captivation that would make him the premier John Brown collector in the twentieth century.

•• In 1910, as if to chide Rhodes, Oswald Garrison Villard brought to fruition *John Brown, 1800–1859: A Biography Fifty Years After.* A meticulously researched work of 700 pages, it was the greatest American historical biography yet written. The fact that the book arrived a year late—oddly, the subject was better remembered on the anniversary of his death than on his birthday—was of no consequence. The author was the son of Henry Villard, a German immigrant, who distinguished himself first as a journalist, then as a railroad builder and financier, and finally, again, as a journalist by acquisition in 1881 of the *New York Evening Post* and the *Nation* magazine. He had married Fanny Garrison, daughter of the famous abolitionist. Their son, Oswald, attended Harvard, took an M.A. degree in history, and became publisher and editor of the *Post*—the oldest daily in New York—and the esteemed liberal weekly in 1897. *John Brown* was dedicated to the memory of his father.

It is difficult to say just when Villard began the book. But over the years he had read and thought a good deal about John Brown. After all, abolitionism ran in the family. His uncles had written at length about their father, William Lloyd Garrison. In the same year the book appeared, Villard was one of the founders of the National Association for the Advancement of Colored People. He had begun writing in earnest in 1907. In the fall of that year he wrote to Franklin Sanborn and Thomas Wentworth Higginson, the two survivors of the Secret Six, seeking their cooperation. At the same time he communicated with historians and curators of manuscripts and retained the services of a research assistant, Katherine Mayo, who would travel thousands of miles, visit remote depositories, and interview dozens of persons who had known John Brown. Fifteen months later, when he had reached the quarter-way point, Villard reported to Sanborn that he was overwhelmed by the mass of material. "I have no less than forty-two contemporary narratives of early settlers [in Kansas], members of the Brown family, etc., which bear more or less directly on the Pottawatomie killings and the conditions precedent and subsequent thereto."[10] People familiar with Villard's daily work load, together with the causes he supported (rights for blacks, free trade, women's suffrage, and pacifism) and his multiple philanthropic obligations (the Metropolitan Museum of Art, the New York Philharmonic, the Charity Organization Society) were astounded by his perseverance in this literary labor.

In his preface Villard quoted the Boston litterateur John T. Morse Jr. on the opportunity so grand a subject might inspire in a writer able to do justice to the theme. "But meantime the ill-starred 'martyr' suffers a prolongation of martyrdom, standing like another St. Sebastian to be riddled with the odious arrows of fulsome panegyrists." This was said in a critical review of Sanborn's *John Brown* twenty-four years earlier. And it was unquestionably the erstwhile correspondent Sanborn whose authority Villard set out to dismantle and replace with his biography. He believed that after some fifty years Brown was ripe for study "free from bias, from the errors of taste and fact of the mere panegyrists, and from the blind prejudice of those who can see in Brown nothing but a criminal." Villard went on to speak of the sweep of his research for the volume and to assert that "no stone has been left unturned to make accurate the smallest detail." [11]

The first stone upturned was the family legend, heretofore unquestioned, that John Brown was descended from the Peter Brown who came on the *Mayflower* and stepped ashore at Plymouth Rock in 1620. The truth of the legend was of small consequence except that it harmonized nicely with the antislavery martyrdom of the latter-day Puritan. Villard dismissed it cavalierly on the authority of the Society of Mayflower Descendants. The Peter Brown who came on the *Mayflower* left no male heir, it was held. John Brown descended from another Peter, born in 1632 in Windsor, Connecticut, Villard maintained. Sanborn, having established the *Mayflower* lineage on the basis of family tradition, disputed Villard's genealogy, and later biographers—Stephen Oates, for instance—as well as professional genealogists have said that the line of descent remains unclear. [12] The Browns were a far-flung English family, of course. Anyone who had read *Tom Brown's School Days at Rugby,* coincidentally republished in Boston at the time of the events at Charles Town, knew that. They were dogged defenders of the right, and Rugby only strengthened Tom Brown's "muscular Christianity." The columns of the *National Anti-Slavery Standard* in December 1859 drew attention to the lineage. John Brown met a quixotic death on the scaffold because it was "in his blood." Thomas Hughes, the author of *Tom Brown's School Days,* some twenty years later published an influential tract, *The Manliness of Christ,* meant to combat ideas of Christian flabbiness. John Brown exemplified the ideal. Hughes compared his death on the scaffold to Christ's on the cross, and said, "There is no recorded end of life that I know of more entirely brave and manly than this one of Captain Brown's."[13]

Brown's early life was still so little known that Villard began where Sanborn had begun, with the subject's autobiographical letter to young Frank P. Stearns. He underscored the resemblance between the son, John, and the father, Owen. Both were trained in "'the school of adversity'"; they shared the same calling, the same orthodox Congregationalism, the same relentless determination, finally the same abolitionist zeal. Two of Brown's children, Anne and Salmon, still lived, and they, together with grandchildren, in-laws, and acquaintances, were an endless fount of testimony, some of it contradictory. Villard was skeptical of all recollective oral evidence. Thus he declined to use the testimony of the Reverend Edward Brown, a cousin, about Brown's solemn oath against slavery after Lovejoy's martyrdom in 1837. Later acknowledging that Brown was in Hudson at the time and might have said what was attributed to him, the author added, "But undocumented recollections are a trap a wary historian must usually shun."[14] Nevertheless, on matters of lesser import the author made liberal use of them. The image of the man was thus filled up. The indefatigable Katherine Mayo came up with the story of a runaway slave whom John Brown, a mere stripling, with his adopted brother, Levi Blakesley, had fed and sheltered.

"I found him [the fugitive] behind a log," Brown later recalled, "and I heard his heart thumping before I reached him. At that I vowed eternal enmity to slavery." The story was narrated by Blakesley's daughter in 1908.[15]

As for his subject's character as a businessman, Villard gave Brown credit for self-assurance, application, and probity. During his decade in western Pennsylvania, he was much admired both for his business sense and for his civic leadership. It became almost a proverb, said Villard, quoting one who had known him in Richmond, "'to be as enterprising and honest as John Brown, and as useful to the county.'"[16] Back in Ohio, his business fortunes plummeted in 1837. Villard counted twenty-one lawsuits in which Brown was a defendant over a period of twenty years, most of them for recovery of money he had borrowed to finance real estate speculations. Although an able wool grower and merchant, Brown had a streak of stubbornness that led him to failure. Villard tracked down Aaron Erickson, author of the damning letter to Governor Wise asking him to lift the sentence of death on grounds of insanity, as proved by his disastrous English venture in 1849. Sanborn had dismissed Erickson as an imposter; but Villard identified him, long since deceased, as a highly respected wool merchant and citizen of Rochester, New York, for sixty years.[17]

A crucial question for the Brown biographer was: When did he resolve to mount an attack on slavery? The children did not agree on this point; Villard finally settled on an equivocal "before 1840." Until then there was only "a family agreement to oppose slavery, without specification as to the precise method of assault." John Brown Jr., who was then nineteen, thought his father had first decided on "the subterranean pass way" plan in the Appalachians in 1840, when he surveyed the lands belonging to Oberlin College in western Virginia. At the same time he had arranged to acquire a thousand acres of this land with the intent of settling there, but the deal lapsed because of his procrastination, Villard said.[18] In any event, Frederick Douglass, meeting Brown at Springfield, was the first person outside the family to whom Brown confided the Virginia plan. Meanwhile, the merchant-abolitionist gave his attention to aiding free blacks and arousing them from lethargy. To this end he formed the League of Gileadites, which existed mostly in the founder's mind. Annie Brown Adams, whom Mayo interviewed after a heroic journey by water, rail, and stage, at Annie's home in Petrolia, California, said she first learned of the plan to raid Harpers Ferry in 1854, when she was eleven years old. At other times, however, her father mentioned other places; and Annie's brother Salmon agreed. The testimony gained credence, Villard thought, when he learned that in 1854 Brown declined to follow his sons to fight and settle in Kansas. He would not say nay to them, he wrote to John Jr., "but I feel committed to operate in another part of the field."[19]

In the end, however, Brown did follow his six grown sons to Kansas. For several years he shuttled back and forth between North Elba and Ohio, where he was still in partnership with Simon Perkins. Finally getting clear of the business, he was taken up with the challenge of pioneering in the Adirondack wilderness, Villard said, until a chronic restlessness returned to haunt him. "He was now bowed and rapidly turning gray; to every one's lips the adjective 'old' leaped as they saw him." It was a mark not of senility but of "the fires consuming within" to destroy the monster slavery.

> The metamorphosis was now complete. The staid, sombre merchant and patriarchal family-head was ready to become John Brown of Osawatomie, at the mere mention of whose name Border Ruffians and swashbuckling adherents of the institution of slavery trembled and often fled. Kansas gave John Brown the opportunity to test himself as a guerrilla leader for which he had longed; for no other purpose did he proceed to the Territory; to become a settler there, as he had hoped to in Virginia in 1840, was furthest from his thoughts. Leadership came readily to him; to those who fell under his sway, it seemed as natural that he should become the com-

mander as that there should be a President in Washington. Even those who walked not in his ways respected him as a captain of grim determination, of iron will.

So subordinate was that will to its ego that one might doubt whether Brown had nerves. Yet this man was strangely a product of the rural life of petty trade. The secret of the riddle, Villard continued, lay not in a Puritan heritage or in a robust imagination, though Brown had both.

> To all these powers of an intense nature were added the driving force of a mighty and unselfish purpose, and the readiness to devote himself to the welfare of others. . . . The essentially ennobling feature of John Brown's career, that which enabled him to draw men to him as if by a magnet, was his willingness to suffer for others— in short, the straightforward unselfishness of the man.[20]

Central to Villard's treatment of Brown's career in Kansas was the Pottawatomie Massacre. It had, of course, been revived, disputed, and bandied about a good deal during the last quarter-century. Villard made some corrections, filled in some gaps, but added nothing essential to the story. Readers were impressed, however, by his conscientious wrestling with the moralities of this shattering event. The author's principled pacifism made it impossible for him to offer any apology for the killings. After visiting Kansas, Mayo wrote that the mists that had clouded her thinking about Brown seemed to dissipate and she saw him clearly for the first time. Villard replied, "I confess that I have moments when I am not as clear," but he hoped for the same result. He felt sure that the captain had not fired a shot in the killing, "if only for the reason that I do not think the whole family could have lied so frequently and so consistently."[21] At the same time, he could not doubt that Brown was the author of the blow at Dutch Henry's Crossing. He shared the opinion of Charles Robinson that Brown was the only Free Stater who "had the nerve to strike it." Robinson, of course, had endorsed the bloody work for a quarter-century after the event. Villard wrote teasingly to Mayo, "If you could prove Robinson's complicity in the Pottawatomie murders, that would be a wonderful achievement." Some Kansans had suspected as much, though Brown never hinted at it. Nor did Villard in his book, but he asserted that the governor's account had been so disingenuous about Brown and Pottawatomie as "to carry its own condemnation with it." Doubtless there had been provocations for the killings, but nothing remotely justified them; besides, said Villard, they did not check but ignited violence. Conceived as a war measure, to set men at each other's throat, they were successful; and they were consistent with Brown's biblical doctrine, "without the shedding of blood there is no remission of sin."[22]

The killings made Brown a hero as well as a figure of terror. "Old John Brown's name was equal to an army with banners," Villard quoted one of his followers. The Missourians' General John W. Reid reported Brown's death in the Battle of Osawatomie. Alas, wish was father to the thought. Five weeks later Brown left Kansas. "History will give your name a proud place on her pages," Robinson wrote in a fulsome letter, "and posterity will pay homage to your heroism in the cause of God and Humanity."[23] The struggle for Kansas was drawing to a close. In the thirteen-month period ending on December 1, 1856, Villard reported, approximately 200 people had lost their lives in Bleeding Kansas. Emigrant aid societies, Sharps rifles, and John Brown did not make Kansas free, he concluded. Rather, "climate and soil fought in Kansas on the side of the Free State men." Geographical determinism so unequivocally asserted might be thought an affront to abolitionism. Brown's deeds, the bad with the good, Villard allowed, appealed strongly to the imagination of the people of the North.

> Like a relentless Highland chieftain of old, he appeared to personify indomitable, unswerving resistance to the forces of slavery. To those Free Soilers who believed in the argumentative methods of the Old Testament, his name was henceforth one to conjure with.

Not in his methods, however, but in his uncompromising hostility to that human bondage for which he was ready to sacrifice his life, lies his undoubted claim to a place in the history of Kansas and of the Nation.[24]

The whole of Brown's experience in Kansas, as Villard recounted it, was chiefly important not for Kansas but for the subsequent raid at Harpers Ferry. Increasingly, though under cover of Kansas, the captain turned his thoughts to the Virginia mountains and the campaign he meant to launch there. He traveled a good deal, to raise money, consult with supporters, enlist recruits, make plans, deliver occasional speeches, and so forth. Villard's record of Brown's movements in 1858 lists thirty-five places, some of them visited more than once. The previous fall he had stationed Hugh Forbes in Iowa. A "suave adventurer" who had fought with Garibaldi in Italy and who inspired Brown to imagine himself "the Garibaldi of a revolution against slavery," Forbes was given the job of training recruits. The relationship proved disastrous, however. Villard called Forbes "the evil genius" of the Virginia enterprise.

The Chatham convention occurred in the spring. It was a disappointment, Villard said; Brown, however, threw over the proceeding an air of fantasy. Twelve of the delegates were white friends of Brown, among his recruits; thirty-four were black, of whom only Osborn P. Anderson fought at Harpers Ferry. In his opening speech Brown declared his belief that "upon the first intimation of a plan formed for the liberties of the slaves, they would immediately rise all over the Southern States." Many would flock to the mountains to join him and become soldiers for freedom. The convention was all very earnest, Villard said; and while Brown's plan of government was wholly impractical, it contained some admirable principles. The Chatham constitution's preamble defined slavery as war and postulated the entire existence of the United States as "none other than a most barbarous, unprovoked, and unjustifiable War of one portion of its citizens upon another portion." Yet the provisional government retained the flag of the United States and repudiated any idea of dislodging the federal government. Villard considered the whole situation anomalous. "The radical Abolitionists openly worked for disunion by peaceful means and refused to make use of their rights as citizens; John Brown sought to oppose the authority of the Union by force of arms, while denying that any could construe his actions as treason or disloyalty."[25]

The raid at Harpers Ferry was an often-told story when Villard undertook to retell it through the life of its commander. His account, running to 200 pages, was the longest and most detailed yet written. Brown enlisted his first recruits in Kansas. The very first, John Cook, went forth to scout out the ground around Harpers Ferry, and found a wife as well as employment in the town. Nearby Kennedy Farm became Brown's command post. Daughter Annie, who with her sister-in-law Martha came to keep house for the men, furnished Villard with copious recollections. Of the impulsive Cook she wrote, "Father lived in constant fear that [he] would make a confidant of some-one who could betray us, all that summer."[26] Brave and loyal though Cook was, he later charged in the confession he gave the court in Charles Town that the captain had deceived him on the readiness of the slaves to rise and therefore on the feasibility of the invasion. Douglass, of course, had refused Brown, seeing the plan as "a perfect steel trap." Very likely some, perhaps most, of those assembled at Kennedy Farm were of the same opinion. Brown himself was disappointed in the number of recruits, just over twenty, who actually showed up. Some of the earliest—Richard Realf, George B. Gill, Richard Hinton—simply disappeared, and the cadre of Canadian blacks, so prominent in the Chatham convention, never materialized, doubtless in part because of the year's delay caused by Forbes's betrayal. Nevertheless, the little band of conspirators at Kennedy Farm kept faith with their leader, remarkable testimony to his strength of conviction and his magnetism. One day, Villard wrote, while Annie was alone with her brother Owen in the yard, he looked up and remarked, "'If we succeed, some day there will be a United

States flag over this house. If we do not, it will be considered a den of land pirates and thieves.'" In these words Villard heard a note of impending doom. The arsenal venture *was* a death trap, yet Brown and his men were ready to sacrifice their lives on the altar of liberty.[27]

The biographer could find no clear purpose in John Brown's plan of attack on the Sabbath evening of October 16. Indeed, he seemed "bent on violating every military principle." He placed a river between himself and his base of supplies, the farm, which was also his surest refuge should things go wrong. He must have realized he would quickly face a superior force, yet he had fixed no time or place for retreat. If the intent was to incite insurrection among the slaves, Villard wrote, Brown had come to the wrong place. There were few slaves at Harpers Ferry; most of the 3,000 residents were mechanics from the North. Ironically, the first casualty in the town was a free black, Hayward Shepherd, a railroad worker. Villard was appalled by the ensuing bloodshed on both sides. The death toll included two of Brown's sons, Oliver and Watson. The latter's last moments were described twenty years later by a South Carolinian, C. W. Tayleure, who told the story to John Brown Jr. "It is impossible," he wrote,

> not to feel respect for men who offer up their lives in support of their convictions, and the earnestness of my respect I put on record in a Baltimore paper the day succeeding the event. I gave your brother a cup of water to quench his thirst. . . . He was very calm, and of a tone and look very gentle. The look with which he searched my heart I can never forget. . . . I asked him, "What brought you here?" He replied, very patiently, "Duty, sir."

The captain's faithful lieutenant, John H. Kagi, urged him to flee to the mountains while there was still a chance. But Brown dallied, for reasons Villard could not explain; at any rate, the delay was fatal to his prospects. Retreat to the mountains was at the forefront of his plan. God had created those mountains as the passport to freedom of fugitive slaves. It was a good plan. The fault was in the execution. Reading Villard's account, one is led to believe that it was the act of invasion itself, together with the sacrifice, that was important to Brown, regardless of whether the battle was won or lost. On Tuesday, October 18, Colonel Robert E. Lee arrived and forced Brown's surrender. How eminently fitting, the biographer wrote, "since the raid on Harpers Ferry itself was to be in its every aspect a prologue to 1861."[28]

Villard concurred in the common judgment that the captain's trial in Judge Richard Parker's court at Charles Town was, on balance, fair and just. Its haste was regrettable, yet understandable in the circumstances; and Brown was marvelously favored by the judge's one-month reprieve of sentence of death. The convicted man's stoic demeanor during that month, together with his numerous letters, embellished the martyr legend. While Brown was no grammarian, his writings were deserving of the praise Emerson accorded them, Villard thought; indeed, "the Browns have all had the gift of earnest and moving English." On the question of the offender's mental state, the biographer wrote, Governor Wise was correct. "No lunatic ever penned such elevated and high-minded epistles." Monomania was another matter. But much of human progress the world over has been made by men and women obsessed with one idea. "If John Brown was the victim of an *idée fixe,* so was Martin Luther, and so were all the martyrs to freedom and faith," Villard wrote. Still, after fifty years, it was bad policy for the governor to have made a martyr of John Brown, unless he chose to hasten disunion and bloodshed.[29]

By Villard's own account, however, Governor Wise was moved, in part, by rumored rescue attempts likely to prolong the danger Brown had started. The hangman's noose had been prepared not only for the commander but for all the captive survivors. The hangings went on over some three months. Brown, it may be recalled, opposed any rescue attempt on his own behalf. His reluctance did not deter the efforts of his friends, chiefly in Massachusetts and Ohio. In Boston the abolitionist Lysander Spooner concocted a plan to kidnap Governor Wise and hold him hostage for the life of Brown and his comrades. "That so buccaneering a scheme, worthy of the imagination of a Marryat or a Cooper," Villard wrote, "should have been seriously considered by sober-minded Boston men in the middle of the nineteenth century, shows clearly how rapidly the 'irrepressible conflict' was approaching."[30] The last of the rescue attempts, bravely undertaken by Thomas Wentworth Higginson and James Montgomery, the Kansas warrior, to save the lives of Aaron Dwight Stevens and Albert Hazlett, had finally to be abandoned, and they died on the gallows March 16, 1860.

In the end, Villard was fascinated by the shock the Harpers Ferry raid and its sequel gave to John Brown's accessories before the fact, the Secret Six in Massachusetts and New York. "Its members were plainly unaware that to support a forcible attack upon a system, however iniquitous, in a country founded on the principle that differences of opinion must be settled by the ballot, carries with it both heavy responsibilities and grave personal danger."[31] Three of them—Sanborn, Howe, and Stearns—as earlier noted, fled to Canada; Gerrit Smith entered an insane asylum; and Theodore Parker, on a futile search for health in Europe, evaded the torment. Only Higginson, the Worcester reformer, behaved honorably, in Villard's judgment, and he had the good fortune to be overlooked by Senator Mason's investigating committee.

The biographer was especially hard on Dr. Samuel Gridley Howe, the renowned humanitarian. On November 14 Howe issued a card—that is, a public explanation—that Villard pronounced "inexplicable." Named an accomplice in the raid by John Cook, Howe said, "That event was unforeseen and unexpected by me. . . . It is still, to me, a mystery, and a marvel." He concluded that, facing the prospect of extradition and trial in Virginia, he must seek refuge abroad. Villard had published his own astonished response to Howe's denial in a letter to the *Nation,* signed "V," a year before his book appeared. "How a man, at other times honorable, could have penned this card remains a mystery," he wrote. For at least a year the good doctor had been fully cognizant of Brown's invasion plan, except for the exact time and place. Sanborn was on record as witness to that fact. After seeing Howe's card, Higginson reminded him that, upon first news of the attack, he had written him that it would be "extreme baseness" in them to deny complicity in it, and in response Howe declined any such intention and said they should make *no* statements. "What am I that I should judge you?" Higginson continued in some anguish. "But Gerrit Smith's insanity—and your letter [card]—are to me the only two sad results of the whole affair. You disclaim knowledge not only of the exact time and place, but of the enterprise itself." Villard had found the letter in Higginson's personal papers in the Boston Public Library. It had not been sent, but another of the same import was. Sanborn, informed of Higginson's opinion, disagreed: "I don't see why it is any worse to conceal the facts now than before the outbreak, provided that Brown and his men do not suffer by such concealment. What has been prudence is prudence still and may be for years to come." Writing to Villard fifty years after the fact, he labeled the article unfair as well as "ineffective." Howe's character was beyond reproach, and Sanborn lectured the author against trampling on the graves of heroes. Villard replied, "From the beginning I have had no hope that my book will appeal to you as other than 'ineffective.' That is because we have such different points of view." He declared he was interested in historical truth alone; Sanborn was a hero-worshiper. But as for treading on dead men's graves, had not Sanborn himself earlier trod on Gerrit Smith's? In fact, he had retold the story of Smith's obfuscation and denial in his recollections, published in 1909.[32]

But to return to Howe: He replied to Higginson two months later in what the latter called "a pitiful attempt to defend his course," taking the position that if it appeared John Brown acted alone, he might save his life. Most of the agonizing story found its place in Villard's biography. After its publication, Henry M. Howe, a son, took vigorous exception to Villard's censure of his father and pressed his apology of acting to shield Brown. Throughout, his son maintained, Howe acted consistently with his character as "a knight errant." Villard replied that the apology was "a deception" pure and simple. To the end he believed that Dr. Howe had "lied basely," and Higginson, who agreed, was left to wonder, "Is there no such thing as *honor* among confederates?"[33]

Villard respectfully followed his hero to the grave. For in his biography John Brown remained a hero despite declarations of impartiality. Too many writers judged him solely by his faults and errors or thought to reduce him to a horse thief and midnight assassin. "In Virginia," Villard declared, "John Brown atoned for Pottawatomie by the nobility of his philosophy and his sublime devotion to principle even to the gallows." And he likened the inexorability of fate in Brown's life to a Greek tragedy. His true deliverance came from behind the bars of the Charles Town jail, where he learned how inferior a weapon was the sword to the word and the spirit. "It was the weapon of the spirit by which he finally conquered. In its power lies not only the secret of his influence, and his immortality, but the finest ethical teachings of a life which, for all its faults, inculcates many an enduring lesson, and will forever make its appeal to the imagination." The story of John Brown, he concluded, would ever confront injustice and oppression.[34]

Franklin Sanborn, whose authority Villard sought to depose and who openly disapproved of the work, nevertheless found it "psychologically pleasing" because, as he wrote, "your original prepossession against Brown, and your tendency to construe every doubt against him, gradually gave way to the magic exerted by his steady and lofty magnanimity." Villard must have discounted these sentiments, however, since his friends in Boston reported that Sanborn slammed the book at every opportunity. He finally dismissed it in a letter to the *Boston Transcript* as a "pretentious" biography, which was also offensive to Brown's children and grandchildren. If that was all, wrote Worthington C. Ford of the Massachusetts Historical Society, Villard got off easily, "skin whole in fact." "Wait till he [Sanborn] begins to speak of you as 'that person,' or 'a certain individual,' and like phrases intended to point to one whose name cannot be uttered without a shudder! I am one such. As yet you are on the outside of the Sanborn inferno." The Concord oracle, one infers, was not universally admired in Boston. Villard suspected him of stirring up the Howes; and after Sanborn belittled the book in the *Springfield Republican*, Villard begged the editor, Samuel Bowles, to stand guard against more such "offensive slurs."[35]

The reviews of Villard's book were generally laudatory. Some were perceptive or interesting because of the source. William Dean Howells, the Ohio-born novelist who had grown up in such Western Reserve towns as Ashtabula and Jefferson, and revered John Brown's memory all his life, wrote appreciatively of the book in the *North American Review*. He thought Villard pharisaical in his judgment on Brown at Pottawatomie, yet acknowledged that it forced him to reexamine his own preconceptions. Now that deed must forever throw its shadow across the scaffold. In the end, the hero was more important for what he suffered than for what he did. "His whole attitude was one to inspire reverence." The editors paired the review with one by Henry Watterson, the Kentucky journalist, who had not a shred of sympathy for Brown.[36]

The review most looked for was the one in the *Atlantic Monthly*, all the more eagerly when the author was John T. Morse Jr., himself an American biographer. He had, coincidentally, reviewed Sanborn's *Life and Letters of John Brown* in 1886 in the same place. In his review he said that the Seer of Concord had "overwhelmed Brown's simple, noble memory beneath torrents of wild, extravagant admiration." Morse was not a man enthralled by the personality or the historical importance of John Brown. He recalled James Ford Rhodes's prophecy that a century would pass before his measure could be taken. Yet here it was. With the temperate and humble purpose of a modern historian to tell the exact truth, Morse wrote, Villard had given readers John Brown just as he was in flesh and spirit and left it to them to judge him. Morse thought the question of Brown's insanity deserved more consideration. And he could not help but wonder—one of the tantalizing ifs of history—if the U.S. Marines commander Lieutenant Green had worn his cavalry saber rather than his light dress sword on the day he struck John Brown, and so had killed him, how history would have been changed. But Morse concluded, unaccountably, that "everything would have happened just as in fact it did happen," a sweeping declaration of historical determinism. In conclusion, however, he agreed with Villard's estimate of the hero. "The story has the movement of a Greek tragedy."[37]

•• IN 1909, the fiftieth anniversary year, William E. B. Du Bois, the black scholar and leader, published a biography of John Brown crafted to inspire American blacks. Villard dismissed it as "a most inferior and faulty piece of work." It was indeed hagiographic and full of errors; but a more charitable reader would look beyond them to the author's purpose. In the December issue of a black magazine, *Horizon*, which Du Bois edited, he wrote of the martyr-hero: "On the second of this month he was crucified, and on the 8th he was buried and on the 25th, fifty years later, let him rise from the dead in every Negro-American house. Jesus Christ came not to bring peace but a sword. So did John Brown. Jesus Christ gave his life as a sacrifice for the lowly. So did John Brown."[38]

Du Bois had become the foremost leader of the Niagara Movement, the precursor of the National Association for the Advancement of Colored People. It held its second national meeting at Harpers Ferry in August 1906. At its opening, on John Brown's Day, the barefoot delegates made an early-morning pilgrimage from the town to John Brown's Fort—the Engine House—which had been deposited three miles away upon its return from Chicago. In his address, Du Bois, the Atlanta University professor and author of *The Souls of Black Folk*, declared:

> We do not believe in violence, neither the despised violence of the raid nor the lauded violence of the soldier, nor the barbarous violence of the mob, but we do believe in John Brown, in that incarnate spirit of justice. . . . And here on the scene of John Brown's martyrdom we reconsecrate ourselves, our honor, our posterity

to the final emancipation of the race which John Brown died to make free.

The meeting was a crucial event in the black people's appropriation of John Brown as an inspiring symbol in the fight for racial freedom and equality.[39]

No less important in this development was Du Bois's little biography of John Brown. It put the legend in the struggle of black Americans. The hero's message and his legacy were fundamentally "that the cost of liberty is less than the price of repression." Brown learned that lesson in Kansas, and the author subsumed the Pottawatomie Massacre under the rule. He argued for the "essential soundness" of the invasion of the Appalachians to open up "the great black way." But the prophet failed and Virginia killed him. Why? Because he preached the truth. "'Slavery is wrong—kill it.'" He was right, just as John Andrew had famously declared. He added the straightening rod of conviction to President Lincoln's legacy. "Was John Brown simply an episode," Du Bois asked finally, "or was he an eternal truth? And if a truth, how speaks that truth to-day?"[40]

On the fiftieth anniversary of the martyr's death, he appeared to be but an episode. Among blacks Du Bois and Booker T. Washington tried to stir interest in commemoration without success. December 2, 1909, passed with the obligatory editorial in the *New York Times* and not much else. Villard addressed the Ethical Culture Society and Sanborn spoke at Rabbi Stephen Wise's Free Synagogue. In Boston several black civic groups celebrated with a John Brown Jubilee at Faneuil Hall. In most newspapers the lead story about blacks that day was of another lynching in the South. Why the virtual silence? Irving B. Richman, who had written a monograph, *John Brown and the Quakers,* thought that while Americans had "reached the right point of remove from the Civil War to be interested in it," the contemporary mind-set dimmed the glory of Brown's heroism. William R. Thayer exclaimed, "What a perfect specimen of hickory John Brown was! The generation now coming forward does not care to emulate, but [also] does not care to understand such a character." Carter G. Woodson, speaking for the blacks, said that Brown was now almost universally contemned by educated whites, and he cited a Columbia University professor who dismissed him as "a highwayman and a cutthroat." Lyon G. Tyler, the Virginia historian, who directed his hatred to Lincoln, wrote, "We all know that the North started out with making a hero of John Brown, but abandoned him for the much more desirable character of Mr. Lincoln." Tyler's colleague Hamilton J. Eckenrode commended Villard for his *John Brown*, ranking it with Albert J. Beveridge's more recent *Life of John Marshall* as one of the two best American historical biographies. "But," he continued, "Mr. Villard labors under the extreme disadvantage of having selected an unworthy object for his labors." After some fifty years Brown had steadily shrunk in popular favor until he was "like an occult character in a Rider Haggard novel."[41]

Nine months after the anniversary date, John Brown's name surfaced in a curious way. Former president Theodore Roosevelt, having returned from big-game hunting in Africa and finding himself at odds with his Republican successor, William Howard Taft, made a speaking tour in the Middle West that took him to—of all remote places—Osawatomie, Kansas, where he made a famous speech. Why Roosevelt, a conservative by temperament, would choose to link his name with John Brown's was a puzzle. A monument had been dedicated to the captain four years earlier, on the fiftieth anniversary of the battle; and now it was planned to dedicate the battleground in a quiet grove just outside of town as a memorial park. For several years Brown's detractors had been saying that the founder of the town—the true Osawatomie Brown—was Orval C. Brown, who had discovered a spring nearby. John Brown never owned property in Osawatomie or anywhere else in Kansas, yet his "cabin," alleged, was preserved in the park. (It was, in fact, the cabin of the Reverend Samuel Adair, Brown's brother-in-law.) Roosevelt knew nothing of this local lore, but he did admire the captain's gallantry in a critical battle against overwhelming odds.[42]

An estimated 10,000 people came to the grove to hear the former president. At the outset he paid his respects to the old hero, then proceeded to expound at length a radical political creed that would be called the New Nationalism and that marked his challenge to the Old Guard leadership of the Republican Party. He advocated a laundry list of reforms, from the direct primary to the income tax, and declared among other things that "property shall be the servant and not the master."[43] It was a sensational political development. Roosevelt delivered his speech in Osawatomie because he wished to signal his progressive démarche by association with a historic radical, John Brown. The speech, as Elting Morison has said, "placed him for the first time in the minds of many as a John Brown among the insurgents." Indeed, it seemed to substantiate William Allan White's idea of "a John Brown cycle." Later, quizzed about his views of Brown, Roosevelt said he thought him much like the Fifth Monarchy Men of Cromwell's time, stern, fanatical, bloody-minded, yet one who rendered high service to humanity in Kansas and gave the North the martyr it needed. Uncomfortable with this assessment, he quickly backed off. "I wish to follow in the path of Abraham Lincoln rather than in the path of John Brown and Wendell Phillips."[44]

Kansans continued to fight over John Brown's legacy. After Charles Robinson died in 1894, his intransigent widow, Sara, kept up the campaign to topple Brown from his pedestal and put Robinson in his place. She raised money for a bust by Lorado Taft to be given to the University of Kansas. She paid for puffed-up biographies of her late husband. Then she underwrote two books: *False Claims of Kansas Historians Truthfully Corrected,* by George W. Brown, in 1902, and *John Brown, Soldier of Fortune: A Critique,* by Hill Peebles Wilson, in 1913. Sara Robinson did not live to see the publication of this last vitriolic attack, but it was dedicated to her memory.[45]

The worst enemies are often the turncoats; and Wilson had once thought John Brown the greatest of all Kansans. Now he slandered Brown as a murderous horse thief in Kansas, while at Harpers Ferry he "proposed to undertake the midnight assassination of millions of men, women, and children" in the name of humanity. Wilson also assailed Villard and his book, saying it was written "to ennoble an ignoble character." All of Brown's motives were false and sordid. He was a hypocrite, a disunionist, a cheat, and a liar. He was never what he seemed, never a committed abolitionist. "Brown was crafty in the sublimest degree of art."[46]

In 1914 Villard delivered an address, "Historical Verity," at the University of Kansas. Unlike Sanborn, who had visited Kansas so often that he was like an adopted son, Villard felt strangely vulnerable there. "Let him from afar who would enter into this spiritual territory look well to his arms and place his legionnaires behind him." He knew that Kansas history was like a death struggle in Valhalla. And he knew that Sara Robinson had paid Hill Peebles Wilson $5,000, more or less, to write down John Brown. The signed contract was before him; it appeared as a footnote in his published text. Kansans were too close to the subject. They lacked detachment. Villard felt he had that. He thought the state had a grand history, with many more heroes than villains. Kansas, he concluded, may glory in her Golden Age and pursue her democratic destiny.[47]

5

Kaleidoscope

O N E   O F the marvels of American history was the occurrence in little more than five years of two tragic events that bracketed the Civil War: the execution of John Brown and the assassination of Abraham Lincoln. Add that one person, John Wilkes Booth, was an observer of one and the perpetrator of the other, and the circumstance is downright mysterious. John Drinkwater's play *Lincoln* opened on Broadway in 1919 and repeated its English triumph. A reviewer in the *Nation* queried, "When will some one write us a play about John Brown as honest and sincere as Mr. Drinkwater's *Lincoln?*" Then he imagined the author responding, "'Didn't you see? My play was about John Brown. He came into the first scene and he marched right through to the end.'" As the play opens, two of Lincoln's Springfield neighbors call to urge him to run for president. One of them speaks of Lincoln's reverence for the Constitution. "'That's why old John's raiding affair stuck in his gullet.'" The other nods assent, but praises Brown for his bravery. "'It was a bad thing to hang a man like that.'" He hums the song made about Brown as Lincoln enters. "'Ay, John Brown. But that's not the way it's done.'" In the second act Lincoln drafts the Emancipation Proclamation and a crowd passes before the White House singing "John Brown's Body."[1]

Lord Charnwood, whose 1916 biography of Lincoln inspired

Drinkwater's play, devoted five pages to John Brown, saying that anyone seriously interested in Lincoln is compelled to linger awhile over the contrasting and lesser character who crossed the stage just before him. They were very different men. Lincoln's abnormality, if any, was a touch of melancholia; Brown was a religious zealot, like an earnest Puritan. One was ardent and impetuous, the other cool, slow, calculating; one was confrontational, the other liked to take things by "the smooth handle"; one was guided by conscience, the other submitted conscience to the law. Brown was a martyr from nature, Lincoln clearly was not; yet, Charnwood said, "he too drank the full and fiery cup of sacrifice." At Cooper Union, less than three months after Brown died on the gallows, Lincoln compared his ill-starred raid at Harpers Ferry to Felice Orsini's attempt to assassinate Louis Napoleon. The comparison, Charnwood thought, was inept as well as unfair. John Brown had left to every northern boy a heroic memory, worthy of the coming years of bloodshed and sacrifice and, indeed, forever after.[2]

His soul truly did go marching on. Stephen Graham, an English contemporary of Charnwood, wrote a book about his travels among blacks in the South. It was published in London in 1920 under the title *Children of Slaves;* the American edition was named *The Soul of John Brown.* Slavery, "that sum of all villainies," in the martyr's words, left a terrible legacy, Graham said. He observed the "quasi-bondage" of peonage that succeeded slavery, and the terrors of lynching, yet thought the blacks were on the road to freedom. Graham closed his book with a meditation on Vicksburg, where 16,000 Americans hallowed the soil in the national cemetery rising above the Mississippi River. Last year in this beautiful city, he went on, they burned a Negro to death, "suspending him from a tree over a slow fire." "That Negro is with John Brown and the repentant thief and many another such, in Paradise." The author reflected again on the dead in the cemetery. "They did not mean that the gift of freedom should be tarnished. . . . And John Brown himself if he should reappear would not be sweetened by what he saw happening in the world. His soul goes marching on, but it is still the soul of vengeance and wrath."[3]

Stephen Vincent Benét's *John Brown's Body,* published in 1928, has been called "the boldest attempt in our literature to treat our history poetically." Some early readers lauded it as an "American *Iliad.*" The book of 377 pages found a large audience. Some 100,000 copies were sold within a few months, and countless editions appeared during the next quarter-century. It is an ambitious episodic narrative of the Civil War, told in loose, jagged verse—almost 15,000 lines—alternately lyrical and prosaic. The story is related through the lives of two protagonists, Jack Ellyat of Connecticut and Clay Wingate of Georgia, against the background of stirring battles and other events of the war. Both soldiers experience the brutalities and agonies of the conflict. John Brown is a unifying theme, a leitmotif throughout, initially as the flesh-and-blood fury at Harpers Ferry, thereafter as a ghostly presence carrying the moral burden of the war. He is introduced in book 1 in prayer:

> Omnipotent and steadfast God,
> Who, in Thy mercy hath
> Upheaved in me Jehovah's rod
> And his chastising wrath

The story of the raid, the trial, the hanging, and the burial is told in eighteen pages of compact blank verse, with John Brown's speech to the court inserted in full. Benét poses the question:

> You can weigh John Brown's body well enough,
> But how and in what balance weigh John Brown?
> He had the shepherd's gift, but that was all.
> He had no other single gift of life.
> Some men are pasture Death turns back to pasture,
> Some are fire-opals on that iron wrist,
> Some the deep roots of wisdoms not yet born.

John Brown was none of these.
He was a stone,
A stone eroded to a cutting edge.
By obstinacy, failure and cold prayers.

Now he lies a-mouldering in the grave, yet he sends through his white bones "skeleton pipes of music" that throb hallelujahs from Virginia to Kansas.[4]

The poet is no partisan of John Brown. Although northern-born and educated, Benét is markedly susceptible to southern charms. He recognizes, however, that Brown was a great symbolic force in American history, one that reverberated not only in the victorious trumpets of the Grand Army of the Republic but far into the nation's future. General Sherman marches to the sea and Wingate Hall goes up in flames.

Every nigger's gwine to own a mule,
Jubili, Jubilo!
Every nigger's gwine to own a mule,
An' live like Adam in de Golden Rule,
And send his children to de white-folks school!
In de year of Jubilo.

Jack, meanwhile, makes it back to Connecticut in time to smell the lilacs. John Brown, whose spirit has risen with the mist above the marching armies, returns for the poet's coda.

John Brown's body lies a-mouldering in the grave.
Spread over it the bloodstained flag of his song,
For the sun to bleach, the wind and birds to tear,
The snow to cover over with a pure fleece
And the New England cloud to work upon
With the grey absolution of its slow, most lilac-smelling rain,
Until there is nothing there
That ever knew a master or a slave.

Benét breaks into a bardic peroration:

> Bury the South together with this man
> Bury the bygone South
> Bury the minstrel with the honey-mouth.

And here Brown's mythologized body merges with the "revolving steel" of modern America.

> Out of John Brown's strong sinews the tall skyscrapers grow,
> Out of his heart the chanting buildings rise,
> Rivet and girder, motor and dynamo.[5]

This epic poem, more than any other work of its time, gave the new generation of Americans a heightened awareness of the legendary hero. One hesitates to say it raised understanding, for the poem was too elliptical for that. But it was read in the schools and it opened the eyes of many young people to the Civil War. Literary critics, by and large, judged the book, as poetry, disappointing. Immensely popular nevertheless, it walked away with the Pulitzer Prize in 1930 and in the years since has become an American classic.

In 1953 *John Brown's Body* was revived as a theatrical production on Broadway. The enterprise was the brainchild of Paul Gregory and Charles Laughton. It was not an ordinary play but an adaptation of the poem for dramatic reading. Laughton, the distinguished actor, made the adaptation and directed the performance. Compressing the poem into an evening's entertainment was a stunning achievement. Having first played to sold-out houses in sixty cities, *John Brown's Body* opened at Broadway's New Century Theatre on February 15. The principal players were Tyrone Power, Raymond Massey, and Judith Anderson. They appeared in formal attire on a stage without scenery, sat on high stools behind a kind of balustrade, and spoke into microphones. They were supported by a mixed chorus of twenty voices, singing a capella to a score by Walter Schuman. The play, in the hands of superb actors, held the audience spellbound. Brooks Atkinson, the *New York Times* theater critic, said *John Brown's Body* was "a stage performance of fire and beauty." When it closed on Broadway, Gregory took the show on the road again.[6] Benét's poem reached still another audience through the public readings of a professional monologist, Florence Locke. In 1968 the Gregory-Laughton production was revived as the premier performance at the restored Ford's Theatre in Washington, D.C.

John Drinkwater, who had a talent for "chronicle drama," never took John Brown as a theme, despite keen interest in him.[7] As it happened, however, the first serious attempt in that direction came from another English playwright, Ronald Gow. The play, *Gallow's Glorious*, in 1933, stumbled over the patent heroism of the character and failed badly. It, too, was a chronicle play, and some of Drinkwater's verse about Brown was read to the audience.[8] In years to come many attempts were made to dramatize John Brown's life for the stage, but none was a popular success. One of the best was *Battle Hymn*, a play in three acts by Michael Blankfort and Michael Gold, originally produced in 1936 by the Experimental Theatre, New York, for the Federal Theatre of the Works Progress Administration. The leftist authors wanted to make John Brown a proletarian hero. After all, the emancipation of black slaves had implications for the emancipation of industrial wage slaves. And so it was no accident that the Socialist leader, Eugene V. Debs, had idolized John Brown. Gold had earlier written a pocket biography of Brown for the Haldeman-Julius series of little books. The play, with a large cast, opens on the Brown family in Ohio before their departure for Kansas. (Professions of historical accuracy were to be taken with a grain of salt.) In Kansas the Border Ruffians threaten to drive Brown and his family from the territory. He is in doubt how to respond. As a rule, he is opposed to violence. Even after two of his sons are killed, as the playwrights allege, he resists Salmon's plea for revenge, saying, "He who takes the Sword shall perish by it." Daughter Ruth taunts him: "You wanted to free the slaves but you're killing your sons instead." At length he prays to God, and God tells him to purge the land with blood. The Pottawatomie Massacre occurs offstage. The scene shifts to Peterboro, New York, then to Kennedy Farm, finally, in an Epilogue, to the judge's sentence of death, followed by the sounds of feet marching to the tune of "John Brown's Body." The message seems to be that the fury of the brave is necessary to liberate the oppressed, white as well as black.[9]

A verse drama by Kirke Mechem, secretary of the Kansas State Historical Society, employed a similar scenario but reached a somber conclusion. Brown is portrayed as a willful, intractable man, even to neurotic excess, partly on the authority of the resident psychoanalyst in Topeka, Karl Menninger. Sacrificing his life to make his point, he is careless of the lives of sons and comrades. The play was produced by a national radio network in 1939.[10]

D. W. Griffith's motion picture *The Birth of a Nation* in 1915 had demonstrated the exciting possibilities of film for the dramatization of history. That film was based on a blatantly racist novel, *The Clansman,* by Thomas Dixon. The same author, curiously, some years later wrote a screenplay, *The Torch,* devoted to John Brown at Harpers Ferry. It bore the subtitle *A Story of the Paranoiac Who Caused a Great War.* As it opens Brown is addressing the Chatham convention. He is portrayed as a charismatic figure engaged in an evil enterprise. The camera shifts, alternately, to Peterboro, to Bellair (Lewis Washington's place near Harpers Ferry), to the Pottawatomie Massacre, and to Brown's final meeting with Frederick Douglass. The invasion passes quickly. Brown is no sooner captured than he assumes the role of a martyr. Thereafter everything he does is calculated to throw dust in northern eyes. Brown is a diabolical deceiver and propagandist, not a victim but the magician of his own legend. Compared to him, President Lincoln is "a leaf tossed in the wind." And the war is waged in the vengeful spirit of John Brown. In one of the last scenes two soldiers fall into deadly combat. "It was John Doyle in Gray and Owen Brown in Blue. In the last death grapple they recognize each other."[11] Alas, Dixon's screen play never went before the camera. But the writer was so fixated on the diabolical Brown that the character kept turning up in his romantic novels of the Civil War. *The Torch,* for instance, was anticipated by *The Man in Gray,* supposedly about Robert E. Lee, though it is no less about John Brown, who is portrayed as "a typical Jacobin," and who by the magic of the scaffold transmutes his criminality into the "Blood Feud" of war.[12]

When John Brown finally appeared on screen, in 1940, it was in a pseudo western that shamelessly distorted his life and purpose. *Santa Fe Trail* was a major production of Hollywood's Warner Brothers studio, directed by Michael Curtiz and starring Errol Flynn, Olivia de Havilland, Ronald Reagan, and Raymond Massey. Massey, fresh from playing Lincoln in *Abe Lincoln in Illinois,* was now cast as the wild-eyed villain John Brown. The film opens on West Point in 1854, where two unruly cadets, Jeb Stuart (Flynn) and George Armstrong Custer (Reagan), are about to be commissioned lieutenants and sent by the commandant, Robert E. Lee, to join the Second United States Cavalry at Fort Leavenworth in the roiling Kansas Territory. Both fall in love with the beautiful daughter of a railroad builder. The Kansas troubles are blamed on the bearded fanatic Brown, who is invariably attired in black suit, white shirt, tie, and chapeau. He is "behind every bush," whether it be Osawatomie or Pottawatomie or Delaware Crossing, a free-state settlement he destroys for some unfathomable reason. He commands his own army of several hundred men armed with Sharps rifles ("Beecher's Bibles") sent by the abolitionists. His son Jason turns upon him and dies as a victim of his father's wrath. The freed slaves in the captain's entourage are so frightened by him that they want to return to slavery. He captures Stuart and places the noose around his neck when, miraculously, the cavalry comes to the lieutenant's rescue. (Never mind that there were no cavalry fights in Kansas.) In the end, Brown is defeated and the railroad is built to Santa Fe.

Little of this story corresponded to the events of history. Nor did the last part of the movie, treating the raid at Harpers Ferry. Brown's purpose in this motion-picture portrait is to trick the South into secession and to destroy the Union. Although the Harpers Ferry of

1940 closely resembled the Harpers Ferry of 1859, the place portrayed in the film is an invention of Hollywood. The bridges and the rivers are never in view. The building called "the fort," where Brown is besieged, was actually the Engine House, which sheltered the hand-drawn fire engine, and it stood there still. But the film portrays a real fort, with high stone walls and cannon. It is taken by—what else?—a cavalry charge! The film was more closely related to *Dodge City*, a motion picture starring both Flynn and de Havilland the previous year, than to Harpers Ferry. It was Hollywood's way of saying "history is bunk." After Brown is captured, the film flashes ahead, mercifully, to the traitor's hanging, and Max Steiner's music picks up the tune of "John Brown's Body."

Oswald Garrison Villard was shocked by "this travesty of history," and entered a point-by-point rebuttal in a letter to the *Saturday Review of Literature*.[13] If it was possible for a motion picture or any theatrical production to libel the dead, *Santa Fe Trail* libeled John Brown. In fact, the old hero's granddaughter Nell Brown Groves, the youngest child of Salmon and a native Californian, hired a lawyer and brought suit for slander against Warner Brothers for $1 million. Of course, as she said with a wink, she didn't expect to get $1 million; but she sought and she won a moral victory when her lawyer settled out of court for $8,000.[14] Hollywood returned to John Brown fifteen years later. *Seven Angry Men* was about the captain and his sons in Kansas. Again Massey starred as the crusty hero. But the motion picture was too dull even to cause a scandal.

Now and then poets wrestled with the meanings of "John Brown's Body." For some, such as the southern "Fugitive" Allen Tate, the martyr "who died to set abstraction free" was an object of jest. For others, such as the Reverend Charles M. Sheldon, author of the best-selling *In His Steps* of 1897, Brown was "God's Angry Man," the like of which the country still needed:

> God give us angry men in every age
> Men with indignant souls at sight of wrong,

Men whose whole being flows with righteous rage,
    Men who are strong for those who need the strong.

William E. Barton, the Lincoln biographer, echoed these sentiments, as did Coates Kinney:

The Great Republic bred her free-born sons
    To smother conscience in a coward's hush,
And had to have a freedom-champion's blood
    Sprinkled in her face to make her blush.

Vachel Lindsay, the midwestern troubadour whose verse was meant to be chanted, coupled John Brown with Simon Legree in "The Booker Washington Trilogy." The leader begins, "I've been to Palestine," and the chorus answers, "What did you see there?" He saw Noah's Ark, the cedars of Lebanon, the Leviathan, and Old John Brown with his wife and sons.

Old John Brown
Old John Brown
And there he sits
To judge the world.
His hunting-dogs
At his feet are curled.
His eyes half-closed.
But John Brown sees the *Day of Doom*
And his shot-gun lies
Across the knees.
Old John Brown
Old John Brown.

Occasional verse on Brown often turned up in *The Daily Worker,* the Communist newspaper. Black poets, such as Countee Cullen, wrote increasingly of the white hero.[15]

    The longest—some might say the best—lyric poem ever written on John Brown came from the pen of the New England poet Edwin

Arlington Robinson in 1919. A monologue of some 200 lines spoken by the condemned man in the face of death, it wrestles poignantly with the "inscrutable necessity" of one

> Who took upon himself the work of God
> Because he pitied millions.

It was, Brown reflects, "a sort of madness" that made him strike whether he found the mark or missed it. But it is only from death that life may come in this "prodigious upstart" among nations.

> For men are children, waiting to be told,
> And most of them are children all their lives.
> The good God in his wisdom had them so,
> That now and then a madman or a seer
> May shake them out of their complacency
> And shame them into deeds.

Brown's name will ever be a question disturbing the sleep of history. (There is no metaphor, like Benét's "stone" a decade later, but the meaning is similar.) Let no man mourn me, Brown pleads.

> A man to die
> As I do must have done some other work
> Than man's alone. I was not after glory,
> But there was glory with me, like a friend.

The poem concludes with thoughts on the harvest still to come. Robinson's last line is "I shall have more to say when I am dead."[16]

The most ambitious poem to appear in the wake of Benét's work was Muriel Rukeyser's "Soul and Body of John Brown," published in the magazine *Poetry* in June 1940. She was an intense and demanding poet with a distinctly leftist stance. An epigraph from the prophet Joel, "Multitudes, multitudes in the valley of decision," evokes the challenging time, the early days of World War II, suspended between hope and darkness, freedom and oppression. Brown is introduced in the first lines:

His life is in the body of the living.
When they hanged him the first time, his image leaped
into the blackened air. His grave was the floating faces of the
    crowd.

The poet goes on to say that his true trial followed his execution. It was in the wind of armies. And he could not be free "until more grace reached a corroded world." The hero's life is in the struggles of the living. Images of cities, factories, and pastures pass before the reader, all shouting "I am promise, holding / the stopgap slogan of a thin season." Finally the soul of John Brown is resurrected in those who share his dream.

—Free all the dangers of promise, clear the image
of freedom for the body of the world.—
After the tree is fallen and has become the land.

Lewis Untermeyer said Rukeyser's poem was "a manifesto for her generation."[17]

•• VILLARD HAD set a new standard for biographers of John Brown. The first important life to appear in his wake was *John Brown: The Making of a Martyr*, in 1929, by Robert Penn Warren. It marked the debut of this twenty-four-year-old Kentucky author on the fringes of the group called the Fugitives. Warren, who went on to a brilliant career as a teacher and critic, poet and novelist, later described the work as "a step toward fiction." His handling of character and incident are indeed fictional in technique, but Warren also meant that the work was his introduction to what he called "the dark and tangled problems of motives and values" embodied in a historical figure like Brown, as well as in a fictional protagonist like Willie Stark, based on Huey Long, in *All the King's Men*. Warren is a superb storyteller, and here he has done his homework. The book lacks footnotes, yet it has an air of authority, and the author is young and impudent enough to take exception to such experts as Villard. Virtually from page 1 the reader understands that Warren has little liking for John Brown. This was not only a matter of "Southern defensiveness," which he conceded, but of plain distrust and dislike. The book exudes slurring innuendo about abolitionism.[18] Brown, Warren writes, "possessed to a considerable degree that tight especial brand of New England romanticism which manifested itself in stealing Guinea niggers, making money, wrestling with conscience, hunting witches, building tea-clippers, talking about Transcendentalism, or being an Abolitionist."[19]

Prejudice bars the author from entry into John Brown's mind and imaginings on God and blacks. Never does he acknowledge the depth of his subject's commitment to black freedom. Villard, with most others, had said that Brown had gone to Kansas to secure its freedom under the "popular sovereignty" rule of the Kansas-Nebraska Act. Warren, taking his cue from a casual remark of one of the children, said the old man went to Kansas to "see if something would not turn up to his advantage." Like so many pioneers before him, he was simply in pursuit of the main chance. And with the loot of horses and wagons, guns and supplies from the Battle of Black Jack, something did turn up. Warren basically agreed with Hill Wilson: Brown's abolitionism was merely "a pretext for brigandage." Of course, he did not recognize this fact because he had, with others of his stock, "an elaborate psychological mechanism for justification." Every factual reference in his celebrated speech to the court in Charles Town was a lie, wrote Warren, beginning with the assertion that he did not intend to run off slaves. "It was all so thin that it should not have deceived a child, but it deceived a nation." As Warren later said in an interview, in his dramatic stance the old man had, incredibly, combined perfect self-deception with a certain nobility.[20]

Despite, or perhaps because of, the breezily irreverent tone of the book, it has some good insights. Brown never learned, Warren said, "that all the archangels fought on the side of the big battalions." Such was his ego that he always acted alone. He made the fundamental error of viewing the slave, with the institution, in terms of abstract morality, rather than in the human terms of its practical working. (Here, however, Warren spoils the insight by asserting flatly that "the negro's condition was tolerable enough.") He seemed uncertain whether to admire or deplore Brown's visionary imagination. It was what drew men to him, yet, as with the Jacobins before him, it masked the destructive potential of idealism. People later asked the author if the biography was "an Agrarian attempt to demythologize a Northern martyr." He said no, adding that his association with the Agrarians, or Fugitives, was slight, and thinking, rather, that the biography manifested "a historical penchant."[21]

Another biography of about the same length, but otherwise undistinguished, *John Brown, Terrible "Saint,"* came from the pen of David Karsner in 1934. The author was well known in Socialist circles for his biography of Debs. Reviewers dismissed the book as a compact version of Villard. It was somewhat fictionalized, as in much of the dialogue; and it made too many errors, some trivial, some serious. Of the latter kind was Karsner's assertion that the Pottawatomie Massacre had repercussions throughout the United States in 1856. "From this moment Brown became the recognized leader of the militant abolitionists." He did not.[22]

One way for an author to escape Villard's shadow was through fiction. A fine achievement in this regard was Leonard Ehrlich's novel *God's Angry Man,* in 1932. In all essential details it follows Villard's monumental narrative, yet with the gift of an artist Ehrlich invests his story with passion, writes elegantly, and creates brilliant mosaics of characterization. Both Villard and Benét praised the work. The focus is on Kansas, though as Brown, the character, says to James Redpath, Kansas is only a beginning.

> A little fighting saves a deal of quarreling. There have been too many windy battles. The fight has been carried on by talkers. . . . We grope for the wall like the blind. . . . Aye, sir, bold deeds are

wanted. Not a prophet giving laws, Mr. Redpath. Not Jeremiah with lamentations. But men not afraid to pull down unholy temples upon themselves, even if they go to their own end.

With the license of a novelist, Ehrlich ventured historical judgments well beyond Villard's. Black Jack, he wrote, "was Brown's vindication. Now [after Pottawatomie] his name is cleared among his own people." When the warrior returned from Kansas, he met Franklin Sanborn, as every biographer noted. But what did they say to each other? Ehrlich invents this introduction:

> "Captain Brown, did you go to fight slavery under the auspices of the Emigrant Aid Society?"
>
> "No, I did not, sir. I went out to fight that rotten old whore under the auspices of John Brown."

There are wrenching scenes at North Elba and Kennedy Farm; at the latter, forebodings of doom and loss:

> Down in the kitchen, [John] Cook was sitting on a packing-box, poised for flight, near Martha making a biscuit-batter. "And people think," he was saying earnestly, "that I'm in this because I'm wild. Maybe I started that way. But it's not that now, it's not that at all. I'm in it because I believe in what we're doing."
>
> "Oliver speaks so, too," she said sadly.
>
> "They ought to see it can't be wildness." He lowered his voice a little, gazing hungrily at the dark girl. "Not when you've got a wife home it can't be wildness."
>
> They both went silent, Martha whipping the paste hard. After a while he said, "I wish sometimes you'd see her. She's a lot like you, Martha. . . . Only she's golden. I call her a lark. She's always singing."
>
> "Oh, then why did you come here? Why did you leave her?"[23]

Such dialogue makes the novel read like a film script. It is written in fifty-eight short, punchy chapters, preceded by a cast of characters.

Interlarded is a long flashback to the courtship of Brown's father and Ruth Mills. For a novel published at the depths of the Depression, it sold well, about 8,000 copies. *God's Angry Man* was reissued in a Reader's Club edition in 1941 to catch the new wave of popular historical fiction.

Among literary essays devoted to John Brown, perhaps none exceeds in interest Gamaliel Bradford's. Appearing in *Damaged Souls* in 1928, it was the seventh of twenty-eight books from the pen of this Wellesley, Massachusetts, author. "I was born to write and I shall die with the typewriter hovering over me," Bradford wrote in his journal. This gumption was doubtless associated with his nervous torments, including bouts of vertigo. Bradford specialized in finely wrought literary portraits that he called "psychographs," which owed something to Lytton Strachey but nothing at all to Sigmund Freud. He approached John Brown with mixed feelings of fascination and despair. As always, he felt the constraints of space. His portraits typically ran to twenty-five pages. Brown got thirty-one. "I should like to make a bit of vivid, concise epic, just such as suits Brown better than anyone else."[24] He deferred to Villard for the facts, but read widely in the literature of the legend. "John Brown," he wrote, "is as complex a puzzle as Kansas, and friends and enemies have torn his memory to pieces in the effort to make him out a devil or a saint, where he was neither, but a human being, with immense aspirations and hopes and struggles like you and me. In any case, he was perhaps the most curious example of the intensity of fanatical enthusiasm, and as such . . . has a profound and absorbing interest." In Brown the author found a man as tightly wound as himself, though in a different fashion. "You can see the rigor in his face, especially before it was bearded, in the set mouth, the cavernous eyes, the sturdy chin. . . ." The burden of his life was an idea. Bradford quoted Heine: "'We do not have ideas. The idea has us and enslaves and scourges us and drives us into the arena to fight for it like gladiators, who combat whether they will or no.'" This insight was penetrating and, Bradford thought, might have been written to describe Brown's "damaged soul." He was indignant toward those who thought Brown insane. "Men who reason as consistently and will as insistently and act as persistently as he did, cannot be set apart as of a diseased mind." His only abnormality was the exhilaration of living for an ideal. From the Charles Town jail, Bradford recalled, Brown wrote defiantly, "'Men cannot imprison, or chain or hang the soul.'" In the end, Bradford agreed with Thoreau: in teaching us how to die, Brown taught us how to live.[25]

As Carl Sandburg remarked, "the solving of John Brown as a personality was not easy."[26] Some biographical essayists continued to clothe Brown in noble raiment. One, John Cournos, constructing *A Modern Plutarch,* made Garibaldi, the Italian liberator, his parallel with Brown. The old hero would have liked that. His heroic stature was shrinking, however. Dixon Wecter, writing his influential *Hero in America,* published in 1941, found no place for John Brown. If he had once been a hero, Wecter observed, he was now wholly unsatisfactory for the part. "His homicidal insanity is not easily forgotten."[27]

• • THIS VIEW reflected the hardening judgment of historians on Brown. "Virtually all American historians castigate and deride old John Brown," it was said at the onset of the Civil War Centennial. The reference, of course, was to professional historians, not to men of letters such as Villard, though some outside the guild held the same negative opinion. It was a period of revisionism in respect to the Civil War. To Charles A. Beard the war was not about slavery and the Union; it represented, rather, the triumph of northern industrial capitalism over the backward South. Before these forces Brown was a cipher. To others it was a "needless war," got up by abolitionist fanatics and southern fire-eaters. James G. Randall, in his authoritative *Civil War and Reconstruction* (1937), introduced the old hero as "a grim, terrible man" whose makeshift life was a pitiful failure that ended in "the insane attack" at Harpers Ferry. The irrational streams of thought that caused the war sent up "the gruesome shib-

boleth of 'John Brown's Body,'" a not inappropriate symbol of an un-
necessary war. Allan Nevins, in his great series on the conflict, held
similar adverse views of John Brown.[28] In these circumstances the
failure of any professional historian to undertake a full-scale biography of John Brown was scarcely surprising.

The most important, also the most damaging, scholarly work on
the old hero was *John Brown and the Legend of Fifty-six* by James C.
Malin, published in 1942. It was the product of this University of
Kansas professor's years of research, mainly in the collections of the
Kansas State Historical Society. The work ran to over 750 pages, focused on a pivotal year, yet, Malin said, "the theme was far from ex-
hausted—the study of it is only begun." The copious detail of this
investigation into every dark corner of the Kansas legend is at once
its strength and its weakness. There is no narrative line, and the
analysis ranges immoderately over so many topics that the reader is
at a loss to connect them. Without a doubt Malin is a conscientious
investigator; he seeks to sift the truth by his lights from the mass of
fable and error. It is evident from the first, however, that he has no
empathy whatsoever for John Brown. Nor does he make an effort to
understand the man. Brown's life and opinions, his hatred of slavery,
his feelings for blacks, his religious beliefs have no bearing on the
author's judgment. A none too subtle tone of denigration courses
through the massive tome. Without examining Brown's business career in Ohio, Malin dismisses it as one of "flagrant dishonesty," to
which he adds the picayune evidence that Brown padded his expense
account for service in the Wakarusa war. In Malin's eyes, Brown's was
a devious career of falsehood and bloodshed lacking any redeeming
purpose.[29]

The first of the work's three parts addresses the contemporary
printed record. The local press, both pro- and antislavery, was overlaid with propaganda, Malin says. The foremost national newspaper,
the *New-York Tribune,* was "essentially radical and not to be believed" on Kansas. He had a poor opinion of newspapermen—Phillips, Hinton, Redpath—in John Brown's entourage. Redpath was

"virtually a publicity agent for John Brown." The survey concluded, however, that in the printed record, at least, Brown was little more than "a bit player" in Kansas history. (Some "bit player" to soak up so much ink!) This assessment confirmed the opinion of anti-Brownites for half a century that the old man's role in the state's history had been greatly exaggerated.[30]

The second part of Malin's work, "The Growth of the Legend," begins at Harpers Ferry and proceeds, generally, from Redpath through Villard, with intermittent stops to revisit parochial quarrels and altercations. Particularly valuable is Malin's scrutiny of the writings of Kansas shapers of the legend after the war. James Hanway, an Osawatomie farmer and a member of the younger John Brown's company in May 1856, four years later challenged Redpath's assertion that the senior Brown was distant from the scene at Pottawatomie and in no way participated in the killings there. He wrote his account of the events in a long personal letter to Richard Hinton. Before leaving Kansas in 1858, Hanway said, Brown visited him in Osawatomie and talked at length on the troubling times. He wanted to know how people on the creek regarded the killings. Hanway replied that everyone thought it "amongst the most fortunate events in the history of Kansas—that this event saved the lives of the free state men on the creek." Brown then volunteered that he was an accessory to the murders. In his letter, Hanway added "that no man in this section of the country but feels confident that Brown was the chief leader in the Pottawatomie affair, and *honors him for it.*"[31]

In 1879 Hanway figured prominently in the publication of James Townsley's retrospective account of the affair, and often contributed further reminiscences of his own. Malin analyzed three versions of the same events over several years. Fundamentally, Hanway did not change his opinion of Brown and the infamous massacre, though remembered details varied from time to time. In 1880 he attacked Governor Robinson for his betrayal. The ensuing controversy, which featured David N. Utter's denunciation of the old hero, has already been noted. "Both parties to the controversy," Malin declared, "had resorted to methods of argument that were reprehensible."[32] In a later chapter on Dutch Henry's Crossing, where the massacre occurred, Malin wrote that the key to the targeted victims almost certainly lay in the personnel of the grand jury convened under Judge Sterling Cato in the name of the bogus government at Lecompton. It was this court that approved the warrant for Brown's arrest as traitor or conspirator. The personnel included James P. Doyle, a grand juror; William P. Doyle, bailiff; and Allen Wilkenson, district attorney pro tem. As all of them fell victims of Brown's wrath, Malin observed, the massacre had the appearance of "a political assassination."

Malin ranged widely to pick up loose threads of the John Brown legend: shrines, associations, relics, and so on. In view of his low opinion of the subject, all the adulation was wasted. His opinion of the Brown family was no better. They seemed always to be pleading poverty and begging for recognition. One of Malin's later chapters was titled "The Victory of Conservatism." He meant the victory in the Kansas struggle of moderates such as Governor John W. Geary, Charles Robinson, and Amos A. Lawrence over such radicals as John Brown and Jim Lane. Acclaiming the victory, Lawrence, the Emigrant Aid Company leader, said that the free states must now be magnanimous to the South. "Slavery cannot be extended. Whether it can be got rid of is doubtful. It is a curse imposed by the sins of our ancestors, and we must bear it patiently."[33] Brown's answer to that kind of thinking was Harpers Ferry. Malin went on to note with satisfaction the failure of the legend to be translated into radical Marxist ideology during the Great Depression. He was right, on the whole. Kansas, of course, had become one of the most conservative states of the Union. Nevertheless, it allowed John Steuart Curry to paint the old hero's cyclonic rage on the walls of the state capitol.

John Brown and the Legend of Fifty-six was published in the midst of World War II as a volume in the Memoirs of the American Philosophical Society. Though little read at the time, it slowly made its way into the consciousness of American historians. Ralph V. Harlow, biographer of Gerrit Smith, in an early review, sought to lift the curse of debunking from the work, insisting it was solid, thorough, and important. "The book is revolutionary in its effect upon the place of John Brown in history. . . . [He] ceases to be the personification of the free soil movement in Kansas, and what remains provides little basis for hero worship."[34] This assessment sealed the verdict many historians, especially those engaged in Civil War history, were already reaching on John Brown.

Those who could not comprehend John Brown on rational terms resorted to shallow explanations of insanity. Allen Johnson, editor of the prestigious *Dictionary of American Biography* and author of its entry on John Brown, devoted his first paragraph to the notion of insanity inherited from the mother's side of Brown's family, the second to allegations of insanity in his first wife and two of her sons, and the next-to-last paragraph to the affidavits attesting to insanity submitted to Governor Wise, saying they constituted "prima facie evidence which no modern court of law could ignore." As to Brown's commitment to abolition, it was simply a reflexive response to business failure. Ray A. Billington, in his authoritative *Westward Expansion: A History of the American Frontier* (1949), dismissed Brown as "a half-crazed religious fanatic" who precipitated the war in Kansas. Billington credited Brown with an influence Malin would not concede to him, yet one no less derogatory. C. Vann Woodward, the southern historian, while in basic agreement with Malin, offered a somewhat more nuanced estimation of Brown's place in history in an essay first published in 1952 and widely read by budding historians thereafter. He, too, gave weight to frontier horse thievery and to the burden of insanity in Brown's life; he recognized, however, that these were but pieces of the puzzle Brown presented to historians. In view of the acclaim of respectable northern opinion for his sacrifice at Harpers Ferry, Brown could not be wholly dismissed as a madman. In the end, Woodward took a cue from Robert Penn Warren and accorded Brown "a genius at self-justification." But with the coming of the war, the historian observed, the question was less about the pathology of the martyr than about the "pathological condition of mind" of the American people.[35]

•• APROPOS OF Malin's big book, Villard opined it would only fuel the quarrel among Kansans over John Brown. Memories of the old warrior were fading, however, even in the country he had traversed and terrorized. In 1928 Samuel M. Le Page, a professor at Ottawa University, set in the middle of that country, made a tour of the places Brown had known with a view to gathering reminiscences of him. Much had been forgotten or lost. At Osawatomie, now a town of 4,000 people, no one could help Le Page locate the home of Brown's brother-in-law, the Reverend Samuel Adair, where he had visited so often that his name had become attached to the house. Le Page did find the house of Orson Day, another brother-in-law, which Brown had helped build, in nearby Rantoul; and he spoke to Adair's great-granddaughter, who had no received knowledge of the old man. Le Page traveled to Baxter Springs in the far southeast, thence returned via the old Fort Scott trail, ridden by Brown in 1856. Along the way he encountered an aged hermit, Amos Tibbs, who remembered Brown and even possessed some memorabilia. On the banks of Pottawatomie Creek, where a bridge was being built, the supervising engineer had no idea where Dutch Henry's Crossing might be. Le Page persevered, located the place, but found nothing to tie it to Brown. The professor concluded: the prophet was little remembered in his own country.[36]

After the last of the children, Annie, died in 1926, the Brown industry, as far as there ever was one, came to depend on collectors, librarians, memorial associations, and, of course, authors and artists. Collectors are a diverse breed, though all seek to preserve the relics and monuments of a past they cannot enter. Some persons were John Brown collectors by virtue of authorship. This was notably the case with Villard, who left the collection he had gathered for his biography to Columbia University. Similarly, Richard Hinton and William

E. Connelly, who aspired to edit a collection of Brown's writings, left papers to the Kansas State Historical Society. Holograph letters of John Brown continued to turn up well into the twentieth century, and they fetched good prices. One had to be on guard against fake facsimiles, however. Brown's jailhouse letter to the Reverend Luther Humphrey was repeatedly acclaimed as a new discovery when in fact the item advertised was only a good lithograph copy of the original, which could be found at Storer College. Some wag observed that had the captain spent his time in jail making autographs, his family would be rich. The children, while they lived, were not averse to selling their father's letters and mementos. Thus Salmon, when sheep ranching turned sour, suspended his rule against such sales. Ferdinand Dreer, a collector, it was said, paid Salmon $1,000 for the martyr's last letter to his wife. More valuable than any letter was the manuscript known variously as "John Brown's Last Prophecy" and "John Brown's Last Words." This forty-five-word message in his own hand, prophesying that the crimes of the nation could be purged away only with blood, was passed to one of his jailers, Hiram D. Bowen, as he left for the gallows. Bowen subsequently gave it to John B. Avis, who in turn presented it to Dr. Alexander M. Ross, the Canadian abolitionist, who claimed a confidential relationship with John Brown. Ross exhibited the prophecy with other memorabilia at the Chicago World's Fair, and thereafter sold it to Frank G. Logan of that city. In 1923 Logan gave his John Brown collection to the Chicago Historical Society, where the manuscript reposes today.[37]

The two most important collectors of John Brown materials in the twentieth century were Boyd B. Stutler and Clarence S. Gee. Remarkably, they maintained a friendly correspondence about their common interest for forty years. Gee, five years senior, had been for some time pastor of the Congregational Church in Hudson, Ohio, which John Brown joined in 1816. Although he answered calls to other pulpits in Ohio, and finally to Lockport, New York, Gee kept close connections with Hudson, returning there for Brown family reunions and on other occasions. Stutler was a West Virginia news-paperman, a World War I veteran, and for many years managing editor of the *American Legion Magazine* in New York. The two men, who had not met, discovered each other in 1930 and wrote regularly and often, almost never straying from their common passion, year after year. Stutler was the prototypical collector; nothing touching John Brown was too small to excite his interest, and his home in Charleston was packed with books, papers, magazines, scrapbooks, and assorted paraphernalia on the man who had fascinated him ever since he read Elbert Hubbard's *Time and Chance* as a young man. Gee was more discriminating. As he wrote to his friend in 1952, "My interest is not that of a collector, save as collector of facts," and for aid in documentation he turned to Stutler. He was the genealogist of the duo. Although he wrote on subjects ranging from John Brown's religious affiliations to the scaffold on which he died, Gee's most valuable contributions were his "genealogical sheets." Both men clung to the family tradition that the Brown line in America began with Peter Brown who came on the *Mayflower,* while acknowledging that there was no hard evidence one way or the other and that no male descendant had gained membership in the august Mayflower Society, of which Gee himself was a member. In a rare lapse into fun, Stutler proposed in November 1953 that the Reverend Gee make up a Thanksgiving sermon with Peter Brown as "the character who not only furnished the turkey and cranberries, but sat at the head of the table and carved the fowl, and passed out the succulent morsels with homilies in the best Elizabethan English."[38]

The two men were, of course, faithful guardians of John Brown's reputation, whether the offense came from self-promoting advocates such as Alexander M. Ross, who Stutler firmly believed was a fraud, or from such apochrypha as the story of Mary Ellen Pleasant, a black woman in early California, who supposedly came into sudden wealth and dispatched $30,000 to John Brown in Chatham in 1858. (The story gained currency a century later upon the publication of *Mammy Pleasant,* a fictionalized biography of the woman, who became a celebrated San Francisco madam.) Both men were more dedicated to

Monument at the John
Brown Farm State His-
toric Site, New York

John Brown Farm State His-
toric Site, New York Office of
Parks, Recreation, and Historic
Preservation

collecting and research than to writing about Brown. Stutler, the
journalist, wrote more. In 1952 he contracted to write a biography. It
was never completed, and he is remembered rather for such popular
pieces as "The Hanging of John Brown" in *American Heritage.* Both
opened their collections, selectively, to inquiring authors. Louis
Ruchames, for instance, derived great benefit in this way for his *John
Brown Reader.* Gee, in particular, was cordial to a Kansas newspa-
perwoman, Velma Sykes, who embarked on "Widowed by the Gal-

lows," a biography of Mary Day Brown. It was Skyes's idea, got from a Brown granddaughter, that Mary "was the real martyr." But Sykes died before she could find a publisher.

In 1969, as he informed Stutler, Gee added a codicil to his will leaving his collection to the Hudson Library and Historical Society. The name attested to a remarkable marriage. As Gee explained it, "We had a legacy in Hudson of $100,000 for an historical society annexed to the library. I became a trustee. I insisted that we begin at once to collect all data possible concerning the early settlers." In the ensuing labor, Gee was assigned responsibility for Owen and John Brown. "When I began, as you know, I never stopped."[39] His decision on the disposition of his own collection owed much to his long and affectionate relationship with Hudson, though it was brought to fruition by Grace Goulder Izant, the Ohio author, and by Thomas L. Vince, the town librarian. Stutler died intestate seven years before his friend. Fortunately, his great collection was kept intact and eventually found a home in the West Virginia Historical Society.

Coincidentally, on the 135th anniversary of John Brown's birth, May 9, 1935, the two major historical sites devoted to his memory, the North Elba Farm and the John Brown Memorial Park in Osawatomie, unveiled commemorative statues of the hero. The former was a gift of the John Brown Memorial Association, then under black leadership, which had been making annual pilgrimages to the hero's grave since 1912. Its leader, Dr. J. Max Barber of Philadelphia, had been present at the 1906 meeting of the Niagara Movement at Harpers Ferry, and he often acted with the National Association for the Advancement of Colored People, an organization he described as "a direct descendant of the old League of Gileadites founded by John Brown." The bronze statue by Joseph Pollis depicts Brown in pioneer garb, with one arm thrown around the shoulders of a black youth, the other pointing to the land of freedom. It was unveiled— a historical grace note—by Lyman Eppes, the eighty-seven-year-old descendant of the black family Brown befriended at North Elba,

and who had himself been present at Brown's funeral. The Osawatomie statue, the work of George Fite Waters, was erected by the
Women's Relief Corps (G.A.R.) of Kansas. It bore an inscription
borrowed from Eugene Ware, or Ironquill, the Kansas poet laureate:

> John Brown of Kansas
>   He Dared Begin
> He Lost, but Losing, Won.

Governor Alfred M. Landon eulogized Brown on this occasion.[40]
The elusive Brown (or Adair) cabin had been relocated in the park.

Brown was more or less regularly commemorated at his birthplace in Torrington, Connecticut, and at Harpers Ferry. At the latter place, also in 1935, a dispute arose over a pending bill in Congress
to create a "John Brown Military Park" on the site. The southern historian Matthew Page Andrews wrote in high dudgeon to the chairman of the House committee considering the bill: "Will the United
States flag, which he [Brown] flouted as the symbol of Satan, be
flaunted within the limits of the Park; or will some other emblem be
set up—possibly an all red design, for Brown was the prototype of
our present advocates of violence?"[41] He wrote on behalf of the Hayward Shepherd Memorial Association, affiliated with the United
Daughters of the Confederacy, which had dedicated a monument to
the memory of Shepherd, the free black man who ironically was the
first victim of the invasion. Another initiative, this one on the part
of blacks, to memorialize John Brown was that of the Grand Lodge
of the Improved Benevolent Order of Elks of the World. A half-
century after its founding, the lodge, under its grand exalted ruler,
purchased 263 acres of the "John Brown Farm"—that is, the old
Kennedy Farm near Harpers Ferry—and named it the Elks John
Brown Farm Shrine. In 1949 the black Elks published *The John
Brown Reader,* where the hero was lauded as "the most important
forerunner of Abraham Lincoln."[42] Unhappily, this commemorative
effort had a short history.

• • REMARKABLY, while Brown's star descended among American historians, it was ascending among artists in the years of the Great Depression and the Second World War. No one created such a stir around the old hero as the Kansas artist John Steuart Curry. He was usually ranged with Thomas Hart Benton, of Missouri, and Grant Wood, of Iowa, as leaders of the new school of American regionalist painting. Born in 1897 on a family farm in eastern Kansas, Curry had been trained as an illustrator and would never quite escape that belittling tag. He later studied in Paris, however, and in 1928, from his studio in Westport, Connecticut, stunned the art world with his oil painting *Baptism in Kansas.* Purchased by Gertrude Vanderbilt Whitney, it became one of the showpieces of the Whitney Museum of American Art in Manhattan. Curry continued to paint large canvasses of the Kansas scene. In 1939 an art critic dubbed him the Kansas [Winslow] Homer. Six years later he accepted the position of artist in residence—the first in American higher education—at the University of Wisconsin. A circle of prominent Kansans, meanwhile, including the state's leading private citizen, William Allen White, editor of the *Emporia Gazette,* sought to bring him home. The carrot held out to the artist was the commission to execute a series of murals for the state capitol in Topeka. The State Murals Commission undertook to raise the entire cost of the project, estimated at $20,000, by public subscription, beginning with the pennies of schoolchildren. As a uniquely civic enterprise, the project appealed to Curry.[43]

The first of two sets of murals was painted on canvas for installation in the east corridor of the capitol. For its walls the artist portrayed the epic of Kansas history: *Discovery,* showing Coronado and Father Juan Padilla; *Conquest,* or "The Plainsman"; *Tragic Prelude,* featuring a larger-than-life John Brown; finally, *Kansas Pastoral,* or, in popular parlance, "The Unmortgaged Farm." The Brown portrait was Curry's masterpiece; indeed, it is one of the most spectacular creations in the annals of American art. The gigantic figure stands, legs extended, with arms outstretched, as if forming a cross, Sharps rifle in one hand, Bible in the other, with two fallen soldiers, one in blue, one in gray, lying at his feet. Clad in lustrous brown, hair standing on end, beard flowing, eyes popping, mouth open—one imagines with a shout of righteous rage—the image personifies the wrath of God over the abomination of slavery in Bleeding Kansas. Embattled soldiers gather around Brown; a tornado swirls and a prairie fire burns in the distance, while, as if oblivious of danger, a wagon train of pioneers rolls westward. The portrait was introduced to the American audience in full-page color reproduction in the popular newspictorial *Life* at Christmas 1939.

Praise for the murals was distinctly muted in Kansas. Its Babbitry did not wish the state to be known for abolitionist fanaticism or for tornados or brawny bulls or pigs with their tails curling the wrong way, the latter two appearing in the idyllic farm scene. Hadn't this always been "what's the matter with Kansas," to pick up the title of William Allen White's celebrated denunciation some forty years before? The state senator from Concordia, Martin Van Buren De Marks, exploded, "John Brown was just a crazy old coot. He was nothing but a rascal, a thief, and a murderer . . . whose memory should not be perpetuated." The murals, others said, presented the freaks rather than the refinements of Kansas.[44]

While Kansans pondered the outrageous figure on the statehouse wall, Curry began work on the second part of his commission: the series of eight smaller murals for the rotunda. His preliminary sketches, in which the artist depicted what he called "the historical struggle of man with nature," added to the uproar. In order to make adequate space for his paintings, Curry requested the removal of low marble slabs encircling the walls between the wainscoting and the plaster. It was a small request. The commission approved, recommending removal of this "bathroom marble," as some called it, to the legislature. There critics seized upon the issue to vent their hostility to the artist. His request denied, Curry aborted the project and left Kansas crestfallen. He died five years later. An editorial in the *New*

John Brown, Arthur Covey
Mural in the U.S. Post Office in Torrington, Conn.; Library of Congress

York Times declared that while the Kansas rebuff was the great disappointment of his life, it raised Curry's stature as an artist; and in
this final tribute it said "he lent dignity, poetry, and significance to
the homely stuff of life."[45]

The revival of mural painting in the United States dated from the
turn of the century. It reached its height in the Federal Arts Project
of the New Deal. (Curry's first mural, *The Freeing of the Slaves,* had
been intended for the Justice Department, in Washington, but it was
thought too bold, and finally ended up in the Law School of the University of Wisconsin.) The Mexican muralist Diego Rivera was a
powerful influence. His frescoes for Rockefeller Center, in New
York City, were a cause célèbre. John Brown, as it happened, was
Rivera's favorite American hero, and he portrayed him often as a revolutionary in the modern industrial scene. Images of the abolitionist
turned up, unpredictably, on the walls of post offices and courthouses

Frederick Douglass Series No. 24, Jacob Lawrence, ca. 1938–39
Hampton University Museum, Hampton, Va.; © Gwendolyn Knight Lawrence, courtesy of
the Jacob and Gwendolyn Lawrence Foundation

across the United States. Citizens of Torrington, Connecticut, who little knew they lived in Brown's birthplace, encountered him in Arthur Covey's triptych in the town post office. It pictured Brown in boyhood, as an adult speaking against slavery, and as the leader of the long trek of freed slaves from Kansas to Canada.[46]

About the same time Curry painted *The Tragic Prelude,* three African American artists, each with a distinctive style, painted historical series on John Brown. The most ambitious of these works was by Jacob Lawrence, who came out of the Harlem Renaissance. He had previously executed series on Frederick Douglass and Harriet Tubman, in both of which Brown appeared prominently. All his work was characterized by highly stylized figures, brilliantly colored in strong flat patterns charged with emotion. *The Legend of John*

Brown, to give the series its name, consisted of twenty-two paint-ings, gouache on paper. Most showed Brown with light stringy hair, long nose, and pointed beard. The last, *Guilty of Treason,* offered the stark image of an elongated figure, clad in black, swinging from a rope. The series circulated nationally through the American Federa-tion of the Arts. It was purchased and donated to the Detroit Insti-tute of Arts. Lawrence later replicated the series in a portfolio of silkscreen prints. The black poet Robert Hayden wrote a poem to go with *The Legend of John Brown.* The first section follows:

Loved feared hated:
aureoled
          in violence.

Foredoomed to fail
in all but the prophetic
task?
          Axe in Jehovah's
loving wrathful hand?

The face is not cruel,
the eyes are not mad but
unsparing;
                the life
has the symmetry
of a cross:
          John Brown
Ossowatomie   De Old Man.[47]

Horace Pippin, citizen of West Chester, Pennsylvania, where he was born in 1888, was often described as an American primitive or folk painter. His work has a touchingly naive quality. He looked upon John Brown and Abraham Lincoln as the saviors of his people, and turned to history to dramatize their lives and vision. The three paintings of the Brown sequence, oil on canvas in 1942, begins with *John Brown Reading His Bible.* Here a neat and studious young man sits at a table before a log cabin reading his Bible by candlelight. The second, *The Trial of John Brown*, shows the wounded prisoner lying on his pallet before stern and bearded jurors. The third and best known of the series is *John Brown Going to His Hanging*. This is a wonderful picture. It shows John Brown seated on his coffin in the furniture wagon, his back and bound arms turned toward the viewer, offering only a glimpse of his face under a slouch hat. The white-colonnaded Charles Town courthouse looms in the background. A few leaves cling to the oak trees. Contrary to historical fact, it is a cold day; smoke rises from chimneys, and the crowd of men around

John Brown Going to His Hanging, Horace Pippin, 1942

The Pennsylvania Academy of the Fine Arts, Philadelphia; bequest of David J. Grossman in honor of Mr. and Mrs. Charles S. Grossman and Mr. and Mrs. Speiser

the wagon with its white horses are dressed accordingly. At the lower right corner of this somber scene, with her back turned to the wagon, is a black woman—the only black presence in the picture—clad in a blue gingham dress with a shawl over her shoulders. Pippin often said this was his mother, born in 1834. If this seems improbable, the story nevertheless gave the artist the feeling of blood relationship to the historic event.[48]

The last of this trio, and the least known, was William H. Johnson, born in Florence, South Carolina, and sixteen years older than Lawrence. Johnson's Brown is less the stern fighter than the benign folk hero.[49] The paintings were included in an open-ended series, *Fighters for Freedom*. One of the best, *On a John Brown Flight*, gouache and pencil on paper, depicted the hero leading slaves to freedom. Johnson's folkish sensibility is seen in the large poster-like *John Brown's Legend*, oil on board. Here is the whole cast of Brown's family and friends, painted after the photographic illustrations in Villard's biography, together with views of North Elba and Harpers Ferry, and in the center of the picture under a cross of stars the figure of a black mother holding up her baby to the sweet-faced martyr. *Three Great Freedom Fighters*, an oil of 1945, is a group portrait. Brown and Douglass stand beside Harriet Tubman, their hands tightly joined. This scene echoes, in a different manner, the triad of Lawrence's pictures.

John Brown, the white liberator, had assumed a place alongside the premier black liberators.

> John Brown was there and Tubman, too,
> And Frederick Douglass great,
> The Civil War and what is more,
> The future of our State.

The verse is from Earl Conrad's "I Heard a Black Man Sing," of 1941.[50] (It was written for Paul Robeson.) Harriet Tubman was still comparatively unknown, at least among whites, but in her work for the Underground Railroad, she, like Brown, labored in the belief

John Brown's Legend, William H. Johnson, ca. 1945

Smithsonian American Art Museum; gift of the Harmon Foundation.

FIRST TWO ROWS, LEFT TO RIGHT: Gerrit Smith, Theodore Parker, Samuel Gridley Howe; Thomas Wentworth Higginson, Franklin B. Sanborn, George L. Stearns. THIRD ROW, LEFT: prison, guardhouse, and courthouse, Charles Town; Owen Brown, John Brown's father. NEXT TWO ROWS: John Brown's sons Salmon, John Jr., Jason, and Owen. TOP RIGHT: Harpers Ferry with Shenandoah and Potomac rivers. CENTER, RIGHT: John Brown about 1857, with sketches of the Kennedy Farm, a nearby cabin, and the schoolhouse where arms were stored. TOP TO BOTTOM, RIGHT: John H. Kagi, A. D. Stevens, Oliver Brown, and Watson Brown. LOWER RIGHT: North Elba farmhouse and grave. (Adapted from Adelyn D. Breeskin, *William H. Johnson, 1901–1970* [Washington, D.C., 1971].)

that she had been called by God to free the slaves. Conrad's biography of her, followed by Marcy Heidish's historical novel *A Woman Called Moses*, based on Tubman's life, filled a void. In Heidish's view, Tubman might have joined Brown at Harpers Ferry but for the delay in launching the attack and her own illness. Afterward she could not suppress the question "What if I had been there?"[51]

Douglass had better reason to ask that question of himself. A black playwright, William Branch, made it the theme of his historical drama, *In Splendid Error*, performed in Greenwich Village in 1954. The setting throughout is the parlor of Douglass's home in Rochester, New York, 1859–60. Several callers are in animated discussion of Kansas, abolitionism, and the sectional conflict. Suddenly a lean, sinewy man of about sixty years of age, Nelson Hawkins, is announced. Douglass quickly penetrates the disguise and embraces his old friend John Brown. Rolling out a large map of the eastern United States, Brown describes his plan for opening a passageway to freedom in the Appalachians. Douglass is impressed. He says he must introduce Brown to Harriet Tubman and enlist her aid. The captain exults. But Douglass's enthusiasm cools when he realizes that the project is to begin with an attack on the federal arsenal at Harpers Ferry. That is treason. "It's mad!" he exclaims. Brown is asked pointedly if there is ever justification for violence in pursuit of a righteous cause. "Yes! Yes, by God, I believe there is," the captain answers. "If we cannot persuade the nation with words to purge itself of this curse, then we must do it with weapons." Douglass cannot agree, and Brown, crushed, taunts him: "Have you carried the scars upon your back into high places so long that you have forgotten the sting of the whip and the lash?" And he departs with sadness and disappointment.

In act 2 of the drama Douglass learns of Brown's defeat and the capture of personal papers that implicate him in the crime. Hurriedly he flees to England. In act 3, six months later, Douglass is back in his parlor, trying to explain to friends why he has declined to attend a Republican political rally that evening. Brown's sacrifice has captured the hearts and minds of the North, and all Rochester is proud that Douglass was his friend and counselor, they say. But Douglass responds, "You have me sailing under false colors." He deserves no glory. He let Brown go without him. And he has discovered, as events have unfolded, "that it is possible for a man to make a right decision, and then be tormented in spirit the rest of his life because he did not make the wrong one. There are times," he continues gravely, "when the soul's need to unite with men in splendid error tangles agonizingly with cold wisdom and judgment." In that error Old John Brown has triumphed. "And now you come to me and ask me to play the hero." He cannot. Finally one of the abolitionist's friends tells him of a recent visit to Mary Brown in North Elba and presents a gift from her. It is a last message from her husband: "Tell Douglass I know I have not failed because he lives. Follow your own star, and someday unfurl my flag in the land of the free." The curtain falls as a torchlight parade passes in the street and voices intone, "John Brown's body lies a-moldering in the grave."[52]

To return to the reflection on Drinkwater's play at the opening of this chapter, it may be said that Branch's drama was about Frederick Douglass, yet at its moral center it was about the bit player John Brown.

6

John Brown Redivivus

T H E centennial of John Brown's martyrdom was December 2, 1959. It scarcely qualified as a significant commemoration on the nation's calendar. The *New York Times* noted the events planned at Harpers Ferry National Monument. The historic site had been authorized by Congress in 1944 and placed under the National Park Service in the Department of the Interior. By 1954 some 315,000 visitors had signed the guestbook. Thirty or more acres have been added to the monument since then, including the land where the arsenal and the Engine House had stood. The latter, of course, survived. Four years later, coincident with the Civil War centennial, the monument would be upgraded to a national historical park.

The Brown commemoration at Harpers Ferry extended over four days. The raid was reenacted by quasi-military organizations. Some of the townsmen participated in a John Brown beard contest. A temporary museum offered interpretation. A play, *The Prophet,* was performed in a sold-out theater by a local civic group. Boyd Stutler, who had lent materials liberally to an exhibit, headed a panel of experts reassessing the significance of John Brown and the invasion. The panel divided on whether the old hero was sane or insane, but agreed that the issue had been garbled and politicized. The *Times* reporter of these meager events wrote depressingly, "John Brown's Raid was embarrassing and untimely when it occurred in 1859, and it apparently still is today." [1]

An interesting exception to the hush that greeted the anniversary was the black *Chicago Defender,* which proclaimed itself "World's Greatest Weekly." The poet Langston Hughes contributed a weekly column. He claimed to have written more than a thousand poems since his first in 1921. Finding no other outlets for a decade or so, he had published most of them in *Crisis* and *Opportunity,* the organs of the NAACP and the National Urban League, respectively. In a column on the centennial, he said that just as the War for Independence began with the death of Crispus Attucks in 1770, so the Civil War began with Brown's raid to liberate the slaves. One of history's great martyrs, Brown was a perennial inspiration to African Americans. In a second column Hughes wrote of the condemned man's last speech, and recalled Frederick Douglass's moving tribute to him at Storer College. Hughes made no mention of his own verse on Brown or of the intermingling of the martyr's story with his own family history. One of the fallen at Harpers Ferry, Lewis Sheridan Leary, was the first husband of his maternal grandmother; she subsequently married Charles Langston, of Oberlin, and raised Langston Hughes. Leary's bullet-ridden shroud, given to his grandmother, was a treasured relic in the poet's family. One of Hughes's poems, "October 16," recalls the raid, when John Brown led twenty-one companions, white and black, "to shoot your way to freedom," and implores the blacks, so many years free, to remember John Brown.[2]

On November 7 the *Defender* published a long and laudatory editorial, "The Forgotten John Brown." "His deep convictions," it said, "led him to work for Negro emancipation as part of his Christian duty. He was willing to free the slaves at the point of a gun. And he risked life and limb in a bold attempt to bring this resolve to pass." He had anticipated the course of history, yet history had all but forgotten him. The editorial fell in with the blacks' recognition of John Brown as a white martyr-hero, which had slowly taken hold since W. E. B. Du Bois's biography in 1909. A centennial edition appeared at this time. Du Bois also updated his 1906 Niagara tribute to the life and passion of John Brown in an essay published in a Moscow periodical. (He was not in good odor with the U.S. government, and in 1961 would choose exile in Ghana.) After reviewing the martyrdom, Du Bois asked, "Was he wrong?" and answered: "No. The forcible staying of human uplift by barriers of law, and might, and tradition is the most wicked thing on earth."[3]

Among the handful of new titles that appeared on John Brown in 1959, one proved especially useful to students. This was the aforementioned *John Brown Reader,* edited by Louis Ruchames, a young abolitionist historian. Over half the book was devoted to John Brown's writings, the remainder to a selection of opinions and utterances about him. Herbert Aptheker, the Marxist historian of black Americans, who began his fruitful career with a study of "militant abolitionism" in 1941, and sometimes wrote on Brown, seized the occasion of the centennial to condense his views of him in a twenty-four-page pamphlet. Emphasizing Brown's "sense of class," his identification with the oppressed, and his opposition to the rich and powerful, Aptheker brought him within the Marxist paradigm. He attacked slavery from four points of view, said Aptheker. First, slavery subverted the fundamental principle of the equality of humankind asserted in the Declaration of Independence; second, it jeopardized the existence of the republic founded on that principle; third, it violated the spirit and the letter of the U.S. Constitution; fourth, slavery was a system of "institutionalized violence," therefore intolerable in a civilized society. Aptheker went on to declare "that with John Brown we are dealing not with madness but with genius."[4] So much for the historical guild's consensus on John Brown.

J. C. Furnas had timed his book *The Road to Harpers Ferry* for publication in the centennial year. In 1956 he had scored a popular success with *Goodbye to Uncle Tom,* which he said had been inspired by a patient reading of Harriet Beecher Stowe's *Uncle Tom's Cabin.* It was the kind of inspiration, however, that led Furnas to castigate Stowe and her famous book. He accused her of perpetuating false stereotypes of blacks and, together with John Brown, of befuddling and befouling interracial understanding in America. The linkage of the two names, Stowe and Brown, was not surprising. In 1889, in commemoration of Mrs. Stowe's seventieth birthday, the Boston poet laureate Oliver Wendell Holmes had contributed this verse:

> All through the conflict, up and down
> Marched Uncle Tom and Old John Brown,
>> One ghost, one form ideal;
>> And which was false and which was true,
>> And which was mightier of the two,
> The wisest sybyl never knew,
>> For both alike were real.

They had, in different ways, shaped the forces that led to the conflict. For that neither John Brown nor Uncle Tom deserved credit, Furnas maintained; instead they shared the blame for ensuring "that North and South went into this crisis in the least promising state of mind." Some blacks, consulting their own state of mind, thought Furnas's outlook on the current racial dilemma was colored by his balmy view of slavery as an institution, and flatly disapproved of the book.[5]

Furnas's oblique attack on John Brown in *Goodbye to Uncle Tom* became more direct in *The Road to Harpers Ferry*. But the title proved to be misleading. As Furnas explained in a prologue, he discovered that John Brown had been largely forgotten among the people he knew, and so he decided to change the subject. Brown was disposed of in the first chapter. Furnas suspected that the old man suffered from mental illness, perhaps genetic paranoia. "It was Old Brown's misfortune—or maybe good fortune, since it gained him fame— that his mental illness fated him to carry out the literal implications of militant Abolitionists' group jargon." At this point, Furnas diverted his inquiry to the historical sources of all this "jargon." The bulk of the book is thus devoted to the history of slavery, from its roots in Africa, thence to the New World. That might bear on "the road to Harpers Ferry," except that that history was a doubtful causal force on a man who was apparently insane. After 326 pages Furnas returned to the Virginia invasion, not so much to Brown as to the gentlemen behind him, the Secret Six. Their portraits were etched in acid. Theodore Parker, for instance, was caricatured as "a bloody-minded parson." They were all intoxicated with Byronic revolutionary romanticism; and had they, with their hero, lived today, they would have been Communist or Fascist or IRA terrorists.[6] The Secret Six, it should be noted, soon became the subjects of a stream of scholarly monographs.

In 1957 Congress authorized the Civil War Centennial Commission, to be appointed for a full five years of observance, 1961–65. Funded at $100,000 a year, the commission also raised a good deal of money privately, and its efforts were supplemented by state commemorative agencies, particularly in the former Confederate states. Mississippi, the nation's poorest state, appropriated $2 million, while the wealthiest at that time, New York, voted a mere $10,000. Coming as it did at the height of the civil rights movement, the Centennial churned up interesting questions on the proper balance between historical remembrance and the rising expectations of some 18 million black Americans for the full measure of freedom and equality vouchsafed in the Declaration of Independence. In Jackson, Mississippi, the commemoration got off to a rousing start on Secession Day. Thirty thousand Grays marched in review before Governor Ross Barnett, while hundreds of Confederate flags waved and the bands played "Dixie." The federal commission stumbled upon old Jim Crow when it held a meeting in Charleston at the time of Fort Sumter events. Some of the northern members were black, and they were barred, with a nod from Charleston's mayor, from the hotel hosting the commission and from the celebratory banquet. The upshot was the resignation of the commission's chairman, Ulysses S. Grant III, amid general embarrassment.[7]

John Brown's soul went marching on during the centennial without much effect, one way or the other, on his image. In works on the war turned out by historians and nonhistorians, he continued to figure as a bloodthirsty fanatic. The unofficial centennial historian was Bruce Catton, editor of *American Heritage* magazine and

author already of half a dozen books of military history on the subject. *The Coming Fury,* in 1961, was in effect a prologue to the entire
series. The affair at Harpers Ferry, Catton wrote, stirred profound
passions both North and South. "John Brown was a brutal murderer
if ever there was one, and yet to many thousands he had become a
martyr . . . by the character of the thing he attacked. Unbalanced to
the verge of outright madness, he had touched a profound moral issue, an issue that ran so deep that he took on a strange and moving
dignity when he stood on the scaffold."[8]

Two plays on John Brown made it to the New York stage in 1962.
One, *Moon Besieged,* by Seyril Schochen (a pen name), closed after
one performance. The other, *The Anvil: The Trial of John Brown,* by
Julia Davis, had a run of sixteen performances at an off-Broadway
theater. The West Virginia author was the accomplished daughter of
the distinguished attorney and 1924 presidential candidate John W.
Davis. *The Anvil* is a documentary drama in two acts. The first takes
place in the Charles Town courtroom, the second in the condemned
man's jail cell. The play purports to be faithful to the facts, and on the
whole, it is. A narrator weaves a thread of interpretation. When the
play was first performed in Charles Town, the narrator was an independent observer; in the New York production he doubled as the
jailer, Captain Avis. He voices the theme at the outset: "Sometimes
in history a man appears, pointed like a compass at one star, a man
of iron, an anvil on which God beats out his purpose."[9]

In 1960 the biggest historical novel yet written on John Brown
appeared. This was *The Surveyor,* the third book of forty-nine-year-
old Truman Nelson. Growing up in a working-class family in Lynn,
Massachusetts, Nelson dropped out of high school and went to work
at the local General Electric factory. During the Great Depression
and the war, he was drawn to radical causes, and under the chance
influence of F. O. Matthiessen, the Harvard professor of English,
became fascinated with "revolutionary consciousness" in the American past, as suggested in Matthiessen's great book, *American Renaissance,* and made himself into a writer. His first novel, *The Sin of the*

Prophet, treated Theodore Parker, among others, and in doing so introduced Nelson to three of the Secret Six. The second novel, *The Passion by the Brook,* was about Brook Farm, the Transcendentalist community near Boston. All the while Nelson was tending toward his major subject. In John Brown he found "the finest example of pure revolutionary morality produced in this country, perhaps in any country."[10] All that Nelson wrote on the martyr-hero was informed by the conviction that he was, first, last, and always, a revolutionary. This being so, it was a mistake to view him through a religious, political, ethnic, or patriotic lens. While writing *The Surveyor,* Nelson made a pilgrimage to Brown's grave on his birthday. Everything about the place—the ramshackle farmhouse, the bleak landscape, the towering mountains—was forbidding. The graveside ceremony was so meager it was pitiful. Nelson got into a shouting match with the custodian of the place, Colonel Briggs, who was a proud alumnus of Virginia Military Institute, where Stonewall Jackson had taught, and a worshiper of General Robert E. Lee. Nelson was not the first visitor offended by Briggs. People came from near and far to pay homage to John Brown, the man who sacrificed his life for freedom of the slaves, and they did not want to hear that he was a blackguard. Unfortunately, it would be some time before Briggs was replaced. Writing of his visit in the *Nation,* Nelson said, "John Brown is the stone in the historian's shoe. They cannot ignore him, but they try to choke him off in deforming parentheses."[11] Nelson hoped to change the collective mind on the subject.

Nelson's novel opens in 1855 in eastern Kansas, under the sway of David Atchison, the former Missouri senator, and his army of Border Ruffians. Brown appears in the disguise of a surveyor, a stratagem he later uses to infiltrate unfriendly territory; and so the book's title. In Lawrence at the time of the Wakarusa outbreak, Brown is like a wild card in the deck; no one can figure him out, though some, such as Charles Robinson, suspect he is dangerous. He opposed the truce got up by Robinson, mercurial Jim Lane, and Governor Shannon. His son John Jr. has already had dealings with Robinson. Robinson, of course, represents the Emigrant Aid Company, "a soulless landgrabbing corporation" in the Browns' eyes, and has worked to lift the stigma of abolitionism from the Free State Party. John Brown is bent on fighting. He organizes the "Liberty Guards" and is called Captain. He trains his men in marksmanship and seeks to make soldiers of them. When John Cook refers to Atchison's "big fat southern ass," the captain reprimands him. "I would rather have cholera in my camp than a man with a vulgar and profane mouth." Brown is a student of *Plutarch's Lives,* especially the life of the Roman general Sertorius, who resourcefully cast dust in the eyes of the enemy. "If I had my way I would see that a cheap edition of Plutarch was placed in the hands of every citizen under arms in this republic." No author before Nelson had made a point of Brown's range of learning. When John Brown Jr. gives him Henry Thoreau's *Civil Disobedience* to read, the old man snaps that he has already read it, and it didn't tell him anything he didn't already know. His boys, he says, seem to think the Bible is the only book he knows. But he has read all about the American Revolution, along with a good deal about insurrections from Spartacus to Toussaint and the revolutions of 1848. Wealthy, John Jr.'s wife—a strong character in the story— tells the sons they do not appreciate their father enough. "Why, did he wallop you when little?" "No," one answers. "He made us whip him." He would tally up their sins, the youth continued, and switch them accordingly, but then take off his own shirt and pass the boys the whip for his back. "Why?" Wealthy asks. "To show us that the innocent always suffer for the guilty." The whippings were an oft-told story, but no previous author had explained it this way.[12]

John Brown's worst fault, in Nelson's opinion, was his tendency to overreach. Exhibit A was the Pottawatomie Massacre, the crux of the novel. For Nelson it becomes a case study of "revolutionary morality." After the spring plowing and the bogus trial at Dutch Henry's Crossing, even before the Missourians' attack on Lawrence, the old man is sharpening his swords and collecting an armed party for a retaliatory blow. Young John, who holds elective office in the

Topeka or Free State government, begs his father to trust in the law. You have no authority, he says. "The power of the sword is authority enough. . . . This is war," the captain responds, reminding John that five Free State men have already been murdered by the enemy. Impersonating a surveyor, Brown slyly insinuates himself into Dutch Henry's domain and commits the ghastly deed. It is justified as "a cruel necessity." In Nelson's recounting of the massacre, Brown is indisputably its leader, but he does not himself kill anyone, which accorded with his son Salmon's testimony. As Nelson tells it, several hours after the foul deed, Brown, in weariness and shock, suddenly doubted whether Old Man Doyle was dead, and so he returned to the scene and put a bullet into his head, then reached down from his mount and felt the victim's pulse. It was stone cold, and for a moment John Brown felt "exculpatory joy" that he had slain no one that night.[13] He had, however, overcome "the sin of the prophet," which belonged to Theodore Parker, in the book of that name—meaning the failure to bridge the gap between conviction and action. At the novel's end, Brown returns to the East with Robinson's blessing.

The Old Man: John Brown at Harpers Ferry followed thirteen years later. By then *The Surveyor* had been forgotten; yet it was Nelson's best work. Some reviewers thought *The Old Man* sank under the weight of detail and, as one observed, "a staggering amount of conversation." For all the author's earnestness, it was unmoving. Being a work of conscience, as a scholarly critic said, it was burdensome as fiction. Historians, who might have learned from the book, with few exceptions ignored it.

• • IN 1968 Truman Nelson wrote an extended essay, *The Right of Revolution,* which an admirer called "a handbook of radical action." It updated Thoreau and Parker, with a bow to Jefferson, though not to Marx, and connected the tradition of radical dissent to the civil rights revolution. Writing in the aftermath of "the black uprisings" in the ghettos of American cities the previous summer and the atrocities committed against blacks and civil rights demonstrators in the southern states, Nelson declared, "They are calling out the John Brown in us."[14] That same summer, a young scholar at Columbia University, Albert Fried, was diverted from a book he was writing on American socialism by the student unrest around him on the twin issues of the Vietnam War and civil rights. In a campus cafeteria he overheard two blacks talking. One said, "The only good white's a dead white." The other returned, "Yeah, except John Brown. He was the only good white the country's ever had." "And they killed him pretty quick," was the emphatic response. Fried set aside his work on socialism and turned his mind to John Brown. The book that came out of this diversion was a kind of dialogue between past and present, between Brown and Martin Luther King Jr., between the abolitionists and the Students for a Democratic Society. As Fried's research piled up, he adopted the thesis that Brown's true purpose, formed in Kansas, was to incite secession and sectional warfare, which would lead to emancipation and a restored Union. Thanks to Lincoln, that purpose was accomplished. Brown became as creditable to Fried as to his leftist counterparts in 1967–68. Direct action in the name of conscience was fully justified. Fried's research never materialized as a book; instead, his experience with Brown in the matrix of his own time became his book.[15]

The identification of black Americans with their historic white martyr swelled during the civil rights movement. John Brown was the blackest white man anyone had ever known. The African American historian Benjamin Quarles traced the origins of this modern recognition to the Niagara demonstration at Harpers Ferry in 1906. In 1972 he edited a compilation of writings, *Blacks on John Brown;* and followed it two years later with *Allies for Freedom,* a history of the interracial relationship. It began with "Brown's black orientation," proceeded through his recruitment of blacks, the events at Harpers Ferry, and the hanging, and concluded with Brown's present place in black memory. Quarles observed the frequent linkage of Brown's name with Lincoln's, and happily endorsed it.[16]

More militant blacks rejected it, however. Lerone Bennett Jr.,

senior editor of *Ebony*, the black magazine, said Lincoln was basically a white supremacist, while Brown embraced blacks as his
equals. Bennett wrote a biographical essay on the paragon for his
book *Pioneers in Protest*, devoted to leaders in the struggle for black
equality. His most forthright appreciation appeared in an earlier essay, "Tea and Sympathy: Liberals and Other White Hopes." After a
slashing attack on white liberals who talked brotherhood but lacked
the will to break with the status quo, Bennett turned to the only good
white man, John Brown. "He was pure passion, pure transcendence.
He was an elemental force like the wind, rain, and fire." He was contemptuous of "talk, talk, talk," Bennett continued. "Always, everywhere, John Brown was preaching the primacy of the act."

> "Slavery is evil," he said, "kill it."
> "But we must study the problem . . ."
> Slavery is evil—kill it!
> "But our allies . . ."
> Slavery is evil—kill it!

Brown's transcendent act was at Harpers Ferry.[17]

Proponents of black consciousness and black power—Malcolm X, H. Rap Brown, Floyd McKissick, and others—invoked
Brown's name and example. "If you are for me—when I say *me* I
mean us, our people—then you have to be willing to do as old John
Brown did," said Malcolm X. So much of the white liberal response
to equal rights for blacks was a reflex of aggravated guilt that it was
gratifying to find a white friend free of guilt. Leonard Jeffries once
made bold to propose the "John Brown test" to identify true friends
among white people.[18] Of course, in all the discussion and debate of
the civil rights movement, John Brown's name was scarcely the coin
of the realm. He had, after all, been a-mouldering in his grave for a
hundred years. And, unlike Lincoln, he was not an American icon.
Those details do not detract from the significance of the blacks' in-
vocation of John Brown. In the course of working out their own
black history, they seized upon Brown as a symbol of their rights and

their humanity, just as the father of that history, George Washington Williams, had done. One radical bulletin went under the name *Osawatomie;* another, *The Movement,* splashed Brown's image on the cover. A new John Brown Historical Association took form among Chicago blacks. Some blacks' feelings for Brown shaded into their visual image of him. On the walls of the Hampton University Museum of Art hangs a linocut portrait done by the Chicago artist Charles White in 1950, with pronounced African features: jet-black hair, large lips, flat nose. The figure might be taken for a black man.

In or about 1965, Kenneth B. Clark, the black child psychologist who provided much of the documentation for the Supreme Court's decision against "separate but equal" education (*Brown v. Board of Education*) in 1954, had a recorded conversation with Robert Penn Warren on the country's perennial racial dilemma. Clark remarked that "the cutting edge" of any social movement must be literalistic, "I mean like John Brown." And the conversation between Warren (*W*) and Clark (*C*) went like this:

> *W:* What do you think of John Brown, by the way? Morally and psychologically? Or both?
>
> *C:* Well, psychologically, the simple denigration of John Brown might be too simple—he was a fanatic, a neurotic, a literalist, an absolutist, a man so totally committed that nothing, including reality, stood in his way.
>
> *W:* How do you treat a man like that in ordinary society?
>
> *C:* Society can take care of itself with a man like that, it always has—see what it did to Christ.
>
> *W:* Do you equate Christ with John Brown?
>
> *C:* Unquestionably.

The conversation trails along.

> *C:* Boy, you certainly are fascinated with John Brown, and he is one of the most—
>
> *W:* You brought him up—I didn't.

Warren did not tell Clark of the biography of John Brown he once wrote, but in writing up the conversation he remarked, "It is far from the book I would write now, for that book was shot through with Southern defensiveness, and in my ignorance the psychological picture of the hero was presented far too schematically." He went on to insist, however, that John Brown was mad.[19]

The man who emerged as the leader of the civil rights crusade, the Reverend Martin Luther King Jr., rarely, if ever, mentioned John Brown in his civic discourse. In a symposium at the University of Minnesota on the centenary of Harpers Ferry, which took as its theme "the relevance of John Brown's raid to the Negro problem today," King managed to speak on civil rights without ever noticing John Brown. To him Lincoln was a legitimate hero for blacks, and he begged President John F. Kennedy to issue a "Second Emancipation Proclamation" on January 1, 1963, a century after the first. The president did not respond, but King, in effect, issued his own proclamation before the Lincoln Memorial in the celebrated "I Have a Dream" speech on August 28. His reserve toward Brown was doubtless owing to his deep commitment to nonviolence. Others of that persuasion in the movement, going all the way back to William Lloyd Garrison, had made an exception for Brown. King could not. His commitment apparently did not bar the violence of the Civil War, however.

All three, Brown, Lincoln, and King, died as martyrs. Historians have had difficulty defining the boundaries of martyrdom. Etymologically, *martyr* stems from the Greek word meaning witness, and so it has religious resonance, as in witness to faith. Two studies in the last decade of the twentieth century treated the subject in a biographical fashion. Eyal J. Naveh's *Crown of Thorns: Political Martyrdom in America from Abraham Lincoln to Martin Luther King, Jr.*, begins with abolitionists such as Lovejoy and moves on to Brown. In Naveh's view, he was the quintessential political martyr, though he justified himself in the name of Christ. Lacy Baldwin Smith, a historian of early modern England, offers a sweeping survey in *Fools,*

Martyrs, Traitors: The Story of Martyrdom in the Western World. He observed that all martyrdom, explicitly or implicitly, bears the taint of treason. Thus Socrates was accused of subversive teaching and Jesus rebelled against both Rome and the Pharisees. "But only with John Brown," Smith writes, "does treason take center stage."[20] Brown was a *revolutionary* martyr in both the political and religious senses. And though he did not exhibit the cold calculation of Socrates, he arranged his death in the same deliberate fashion. Smith found room to include Mohandas Gandhi in his study, but, curiously, neither Lincoln nor King, though all three were victims of private assassins.

• • T H E C I V I L rights movement shook up the historical fraternity, firmly established black history in the academy, and caused many students to take a new look at John Brown. Nor were the reverberations confined to the academy. At last, it seemed, the frame of ambivalence that had encased thinking and writing about John Brown cracked and fell away. It was no longer necessary to perceive him as either hero or villain, saint or devil, or some amalgam of both. The years 1970–73 saw the appearance of three important biographical studies of Brown. Together they pointed the way to a richer, deeper understanding of the man, at once empathetic and critical.

The first of these books, *To Purge This Land with Blood: A Biography of John Brown,* was the work of Stephen B. Oates, a young historian at the University of Massachusetts. It was the first full-length life of Brown based on original research since Oswald Garrison Villard's biography, sixty years earlier. Oates still owed much to Villard; even when he took issue with him, he paid silent tribute to the benchmark biography. To him no less than to the earlier biographer it was "a tragic story." Far more than Villard and more like Sanborn, Oates emphasized the power of Calvinist Christianity in Brown's life, from the piety of daily prayers to the conviction that he was a predestined instrument of God. As a Garrisonian abolitionist, Brown was sworn to nonresistance in the presence of evil. The turn toward the acceptance of violence, Oates thought, occurred with the writing of "Sambo's Mistakes" and the organization of the biracial League of Gileadites in Springfield. Oates's style was bland, guaranteed not to jar the reader; but he wrote with admirable precision and clarity. Two well-drawn maps of "Brown country" in Kansas provided valuable geographical orientation. Careful review of Brown's role in Kansas led Oates to a harsh verdict on James C. Malin. The mask of scientific history fell away as Malin was revealed to be grossly biased against Brown. Oates rejected Malin's "political assassination" thesis of the Pottawatomie Massacre, and instead endorsed, with Judge Hanway and others, the idea of a "retaliatory blow" against the Border Ruffians. With regard to Harpers Ferry, the author drew a distinction, not made before, between Brown's "Appalachian Passway" plan as disclosed to Douglass at Springfield and the "second version," for incursion into Virginia. Villard erred, he thought, in saying the Virginia plan—that is, Harpers Ferry— evolved before Brown went to Kansas. The biography was especially notable for its reasoned rejection of the insanity plea introduced on Brown's behalf after the trial and taken up and elaborated by present-day historians such as Allan Nevins. In the end he was content to rest the case on the *Boston Post*'s judgment at the time: "John Brown may be a lunatic, [but if so] then one-fourth of the people of Massachusetts are madmen."[21]

Some years later, Oates authored a valuable essay, "John Brown and His Judges: A Critique of the Historical Literature."[22] Here he was also something of a polemicist. Truman Nelson, in the *Nation*, had damned Oates's biography with faint praise, saying it was a worthy update of Villard but irrelevant to present times. The idea that orthodox Calvinism offered the key to Brown's character, making him therefore a hate-filled man, was intolerable to Nelson. It was like a second hanging. "Actually," said Nelson, "all Brown took from Calvinism was its revolutionary cutting edge and its revolutionary righteousness." Oates replied that Brown was both a Calvinist and a revolutionary, as Nelson would have it. Unfortunately, Nelson allowed his current black-power fervor, together with leftist secular bias, to distort his understanding of the historical John Brown.[23]

The other two biographies of this time were authored by richly talented journalists, Jules Abels and Richard O. Boyer. The former's *Man on Fire: John Brown and the Cause of Liberty* (1971) appeared in the shadow of Oates's book. Clearly stating his stance at the outset, Abels wrote, "I shall record Brown's failings in character, judged by accepted ethical and moral codes. But, warts and all, his story impresses me as an inspiring saga of what one human being, in the evening of his life, saddled with a record of past failure, armed with nothing but conviction, the indomitable will to fight the devil, and consummate gall, can do to shake the national will." If literary style were the standard, Abels would surely be favored over Oates. Historical judgment was another matter, however. Having adopted Warren's view on Brown's light regard for truth, Abels maintained that his claim to *Mayflower* descent—a matter still undecided, in Oates's opinion—"appears to have been an invention on his [Brown's] part when he cultivated Boston aristocracy." This remark was unkind and unsubstantiated. The autobiographical letter Brown wrote to young Frank Stearns, which Oates thought among the most revealing documents Brown ever wrote, Abels dismissed as "self-serving" and designed to win the approval of the boy's father. Worst of all, perhaps, was the analogy the author drew between the Pottawatomie Massacre and the acts of terror perpetrated by Hitler and Stalin—an echo of Furnas. Yet on most important points the two authors were in agreement. Brown was deluded on the slaves' readiness to take up arms and revolt. The mountain plan of attack on slavery, which Douglass, in his autobiography, traced to Springfield in 1847, was actually very different from the Virginia plan revealed to him in Rochester a decade later. Finally, Abels was in complete accord with the Massachusetts author on the insanity issue.[24]

Richard O. Boyer's book, *The Legend of John Brown: A Biography and a History,* made its appearance early in 1973. It is unusual in several ways. First of all, it carries John Brown's life only to his arrival in

Kansas, October 1855. A second volume was envisioned, but it was aborted by the author's untimely death six months after publication of the original volume. Boyer had written a couple of books on American labor and related matters, but he was best known as a prolific author of profiles in *The New Yorker*. There he employed a sparkling style on a remarkable range of subjects, from Lou Little, the legendary football coach at Columbia University, to Dimitri Mitropolous, the celebrated conductor. He labored for years to get John Brown straight, which meant liberating him from the contorted box he had been put in. Second, as suggested by the bisected subtitle, Boyer attempted to interweave John Brown's life into a generous narrative of American history from 1800 to 1855. The protagonist was easily lost in the unfolding canvas. One is reminded of Tristram Shandy's dilemma:

> Could a historiographer drive on his history, as a muleteer drives on his mule—straightforward;—for instance from Rome all the way to Loretto, without ever once turning his head aside either to the right hand or to the left,—he might venture to foretell you to an hour when he should go to his journey's end;—but the thing is, morally speaking, impossible: For if he is a man of the least spirit, he will have fifty deviations from a straight line to make with this or that party as he goes along, which he can no ways avail.[25]

There are many good things in the 571-page text; for instance, a discussion of Brown's personal letters. But Boyer, in Shandyan fashion, is constantly detouring from the biography. There is a little essay on Eli Whitney and the cotton gin, presumably because it made possible the Cotton Kingdom, founded on slave labor, and slavery produced John Brown as well as John C. Calhoun. There is another aside on the Erie Canal; for, after all, "John Brown's middle years were powerfully influenced by the Erie Canal." There is a rich tapestry here, though one that obscures as much as it illuminates. Some of Boyer's insights are striking. When Brown wrote to his Kansas-bound sons that he meant to labor in "another part of the field," he was referring not to Virginia but to North Elba and the experiment with blacks there. Boyer offers no hard evidence for this interpretation, however. What saves the book in the end is the author's infectious enthusiasm for his subject and his polished prose. For him Brown stands at the center of American history. He is Ahab, who loses his life in pursuit of the Leviathan, slavery; and he is the redeemer of "the great family of man."[26]

Playwrights continued to be attracted to John Brown as a subject. A sharply etched drama, *Harpers Ferry,* by Barrie Stavis, premiered at the Guthrie Theatre in Minneapolis in 1967. According to Tyrone Guthrie, who directed, it was the first new play to be added to the theater's repertory. On a stage set with little more than platforms and dramatic lighting, two scenes, the first at Kennedy Farm, the second at the Engine House, are played out. The dialogue is well constructed, often moving. The scenes define the cast, though there is also a cameo of John Brown's last interview with Douglass. Lewis Washington's captive sword receives considerable attention. As soon as the captain hears of this relic from Cook, he exclaims, "I must have that sword!" (Presumably Stavis had not read Moncure Conway's recantation about that sword. He it was who, upon the martyr's death, had invested it with revolutionary symbolism and then, in a children's story, traced it to King Arthur's Excalibur. Alas, Conway confessed in the *Century* in 1891, everything had been mistaken. Frederick the Great had never presented a sword to George Washington. The State of New York, in paying a high price for this relic, had been deceived. Worst of all, John Brown had dispatched six of his men to retrieve this antique at Bel Air; indeed, said Conway, had offered up his whole crew "as on an altar before the mythical sword.")[27] The action of the play adheres closely to the historical record, though inexplicably Stavis brings Mary, Brown's wife, rather than Annie and her sister-in-law, to keep house at Kennedy Farm. The thrust of this intense drama is that the hero, whether right or wrong, was in the grip of a moral compulsion that would let him do no other. In the end, the word eclipses the sword. Stavis later wrote a companion volume to the play, meant especially for producers and performers, titled *John Brown: The Sword and the Word.*[28]

Among the recent generation of American poets, Michael Harper, who is black, seems to have been the most interested in John Brown. Brown is the subject of a whole group of spare and newsy verses in *Images of Kin,* a book of selected poems published in 1977. One is called "'S.P.W.': Journey of Consciousness."

> These mountains are my plan:
> natural forts conceal
> armed squads of five
> on a twenty-five-mile line;
> slaves run off
> to keep them strong;
> the infirm underground,
> property insecure with blood:
> "Subterranean Pass Way."[29]

John Brown's soul went marching on as the twentieth century drew to a close. A pictorial history, *John Brown: "That Thundering Voice of Jehovah,"* by Stan Cohen, made its appearance. Based largely on the Stutler Collection in Charleston, West Virginia, it is an introduction to the pictorial record; but it also reprints such important articles as Alexander Boteler's eyewitness account of the Harpers Ferry raid published in the *Century* in 1883, and offers capsule histories of such curiosities as the John Brown Bell, a relic of the Engine House. *His Soul Goes Marching On* was a book of scholarly essays about Brown and Harpers Ferry published in 1995. Traversing a wide field, from the black response to the execution to the reputed mental disorder of the victim, the book, edited by Paul Finkelman, suggested that Brown was alive and well among Clio's academic practitioners. Further evidence that the legend was alive and well came at a John Brown 2000 Conference at Harpers Ferry.

Two books quite without academic pretensions made their appearance about the same time. George McDonald Fraser, the creator of that indomitable Victorian rogue Sir Harry Flashman, V.C., in the tenth volume of his memoirs, *Flashman and the Angel of the Lord*, came to the story of his part in that "dreadful folly," Harpers Ferry. Flashman's swashbuckling adventures in India during the Mutiny, in the Crimea during the charge of the Light Brigade, in Africa, the American West, and elsewhere, had been chronicled in previous volumes. Now under his assumed name, Beauchamp Millword Comber, he renews acquaintance with a friend, Crixus, he had earlier known as a conductor on the Underground Railway. Crixus tells Comber of the fury old Osawatomie Brown threatens to unloose upon the country. Well, Comber asks, why not arrest him? "Arrest John Brown?" Crixus says in disbelief. "Why, then, sir, we should have a storm indeed! The North would not abide it, Mr. Comber! He is an hero!" Brown, hearing of Comber and his exploits, wants him to replace his traitorous drillmaster, Hugh Forbes. But Allan Pinkerton, the famous detective, hearing of this plan and seeking to save the Union, enlists Comber as a double agent to restrain and deflect Brown from his object. They are introduced to each other in Franklin Sanborn's home in Concord. Sizing him up, Flashman says Brown is "as big a humbug as I am myself." Brown charms his abolitionist friends, and Flashman grasps the magic of the performance. "In his backwoods way, he had great style." The plot is set, and Fraser proceeds to sketch Brown's life. Then, with a scrupulous eye, he describes the events at Harpers Ferry. Flashman, a.k.a. Comber, becomes one of Brown's pet lambs, yet is an unwilling participant in the affair he is unable to prevent. It was a fiasco, of course. In the end Flashman cannot gainsay Brown's bravery and confesses he is "a bloody hard man to dislike."[30]

Fraser's book raises the possibility that John Brown may eventually become a figure of fun. At the minimum it erases some of the gravitas from the image. A year later a historical novel by Bruce Olds, *Raising Holy Hell,* for all its seriousness, has the same sprightly character. Olds obviously knows a good deal about John Brown, but he chose to write a work of fiction "some of whose characters, situa-

tions, and events were lifted from history, reconstituted and rede-
ployed," he says impishly. "And some of whose were not." Proceeding by leaps and jerks, the novel offers a cryptic and disjointed narrative of Brown's life, with asides on the horrors of slavery and
vignettes of Nat Turner, Frederick Douglass, Harriet Tubman, and
Abraham Lincoln, among others. John Brown's voice, in italic type,
provides a running commentary. Of the Pottawatomie Massacre he
says, "*Those killings were calculated to strike terror and provoke reaction and achieve shock value. Thus their nature: the victims—
none of them slaveowners—dragged from their beds on the Sabbath
in the dead of night—I had not forgotten the lesson of Old Nat
Turner—despatched with broadswords, their corpses mutilated and
abandoned.*"[31] The explanation is offhand, and it does not sound like
John Brown. *Raising Holy Hell* is a hard book to take hold of. While
not without interest, it is an exercise in unbridled free association on
John Brown.

The written word was not the only medium of the John Brown
image. In 1996 the National Portrait Gallery, in Washington, resurrected a long-lost photograph of John Brown (see p. 8), which provoked unusual interest. The gallery bought it at a Sotheby's auction
for $115,000. Believed to be the earliest known portrait of Brown, it
was the work of perhaps the earliest black daguerreotypist, Augustus
Washington. Born in 1820 or 1821 to a freed slave living in New Jersey, Washington studied intermittently at the Oneida Institute and
Dartmouth College before opening a daguerrean studio in Hartford,
Connecticut. He was an abolitionist with a roving camera, and probably met up with John Brown in Springfield in 1847. The $3'' \times 4\frac{1}{2}''$
portrait is fascinating. Brown is shown three-quarter length, clean-
shaven, eyes gazing brightly into the camera, attired in black vest,
waistcoat, and stock, his right hand upraised as if taking an oath, his
left grasping a standard with a banner. It is conjectured that he is taking an oath to abolish slavery and that the banner is that of the Subterranean Passway. It may be the most arresting likeness ever taken
of John Brown. Augustus Washington, despairing of the future of his

people in the United States, emigrated to Liberia in 1853 and continued to practice his profession there. An exhibit of his lifework at the NPG traveled to Hartford and New York City.[32]

The arts of music and dance have sought to express in their own terms the life and spirit of John Brown. A number of choral compositions have employed the text of Stephen Vincent Benét's *John Brown's Body*. Perhaps the earliest of these works, *John Brown's Song*, by Robert Delaney, in 1932, is a choral poem for mixed voices and orchestra. "There is a song in my bones," it begins; and it closes, "My bones and I have risen / And will not hide us till our song is done."[33] Dave Soldier has composed a cantata for orchestra and chorus, *The Apotheosis of John Brown*, with a narrative derived from Frederick Douglass's writings. More ambitious by far is the three-act opera *John Brown*, with music and libretto by Kirke Mechem. (His father, of the same name, had written a play about the hero in 1939.) Portions of the opera, dating from 1990, have been performed, but it has yet to have a full staged performance. Mechem has sought to express in operatic terms what he has called the "epochal quality" of John Brown's life, the "religious birthpang" of a nation that vanquished the enemy of slavery as Russia freed itself from the Crimean Tatars under Boris Godunov. The Kansas City Lyric Opera undertook to stage the opera in the 1995–96 season. It was defeated, however, by the sheer magnitude of the score (full orchestra, large cast, and two choruses) and its length (three and one-half hours). The production was canceled. As far as the Lyric Opera was concerned, said the music editor of the *Kansas City Star*, "John Brown will go on mouldering in the grave."[34]

In the dance Ted Shawn, Daniel Nagrin, and Erick Hawkins led the way. Shawn's *John Brown Sees the Glory*, in 1949, was said to be the longest solo dance ever performed in the United States. Shawn took the dance abroad, and it would be filmed for instruction in ballet schools. In 1947 Erick Hawkins, a lead dancer in the Martha Graham Company, performed what was called "a passion play" about John Brown. It employed an interlocutor voicing a poetic text, with a set designed by Isamu Noguchi. Hawkins later revived the dance for his own avant-garde company.[35]

•• *Cloudsplitter,* the most impressive historical novel yet to be written about John Brown, was published to generous acclaim in 1998. The adverb *about* is deliberately chosen, for John Brown is not the protagonist of this work. Russell Banks was the well-known author of a dozen novels and two collections of short stories. Two of his novels, *Affliction* and *The Sweet Hereafter,* were made into motion pictures. In his first attempt at historical fiction, Banks opted to tell John Brown's story through the eyes of his third son, Owen, born in 1824. Owen grew to be a strapping red-haired youth with a lame right arm, able, likable, and a favorite of his father. He escaped from Harpers Ferry and lived out most of the remaining thirty years of his life as a reclusive shepherd in the San Gabriel Mountains of California. Banks, for literary purposes, extends his life about twenty years. He places him at the last great event of the John Brown saga, the final burial, in 1899, of the disinterred bones of nine of the comrades who lost their lives at Harpers Ferry. Owen, the bearded *isolato,* mingles awkwardly with the vast crowd gathered around the huge gray rock that marked the grave. After returning to his mountain cabin, Owen looks upon the visit that had seemed a blessing as a curse. He is haunted by long-buried memories of betrayal and regret. Then there comes to his door a stranger, Katherine Mayo, seeking Owen's story for "the Professor," Oswald Garrison Villard, who is writing John Brown's biography. Owen sullenly turns her away. This episode, of course, could not have happened in real life. Owen had died in 1889; Mayo found no opportunity to interview him. Nevertheless, on this artifice Banks hangs his tale. For he imagines that Owen, on reflection, changes his mind. He decides to unburden himself to Miss Mayo. To her he writes a bookful of letters—755 pages of letters—telling his and his father's story.

John Brown emerges vividly, if not completely, in the pages of the novel. Owen's story begins in western Pennsylvania, when he is a six-

or seven-year-old boy who has lost his mother. He loves his father beyond measure. "He shaped me and gave me a life that took on great meaning." Yet, like his brothers, he could not worship his father's harsh and demanding God. "Every morning, before the beginning of our day's labor, we gathered together in the parlor for prayers and Father's brief sermon, and even though I had grown long used to these solemn services, they nevertheless uplifted me, as I believe they did the others and made the day's work easier, for despite my unbelief, the services connected our labor to something larger than ourselves and our petty daily needs." Owen well remembered that Sabbath day when he and his brothers climbed out on the roof of the house hoping to escape the oppressive confinement, and Owen fell and injured his arm. He portrayed his father as a man inflamed. Increasingly slavery fueled that flame. For Miss Mayo, Owen recalled the family, seated before the fireplace in Hudson, reading aloud from one of his father's books, Theodore Weld's remarkable tract, *American Slavery as It Is: Testimony of a Thousand Witnesses* (1839). First, his stepmother, Mary, read, haltingly; then John, the oldest child, then Jason, and the rest according to age. When the book came to Owen he read: "We will prove, in the first place, by a cloud of witnesses that the slaves are whipped with such inhuman severity as to lacerate and mangle their flesh in the most shocking manner, leaving permanent scars and ridges. After establishing this," wrote Weld, "we will present a mass of testimony confirming a great variety of other tortures." It was this sharing of "a vision of the fate of our Negro brethren," Owen wrote, that made "our blood ties mystical and transcendent." Once in Kansas, the son remembered, he asked his father when he first knew the blacks were as human as himself. His father replied with the story of the abused slave boy he met in Ohio when he was twelve. Owen could not help but link this experience with the terrible wound to his father's heart suffered upon the death of his first wife not long before.[36]

The North Elba period of Brown's life is the center of the novel. "The wild Adirondack landscape . . . moved the Old Man wonderfully," Owen wrote to Miss Mayo. The farm, 240 acres of tableland encircled by mountains, together with the black community of Timbuctoo and the opportunities afforded to move escaped slaves to Canada—here was the place for John Brown "to build his racially harmonious city on a hill." From this point, there is a story within the story about the wrenching moral and psychological difficulties of interracial relations. Owen quickly makes friends with Lyman Eppes, an alert, able young black man his father takes a shine to. Lyman and his wife, Susan, come to live with the Browns. For the first time Owen confronts his own race consciousness. Feeling ashamed of his whiteness, he resolves to overcome it by dedicating his life, as his father has done, to the destruction of slavery. Two fugitive slaves, Mr. and Mrs. Canon, who are John Brown's "cargo" for Port Kent, on Lake Champlain, thence for transport to Canada by a Quaker boatman, stir up a good deal of excitement. An armed slave-catcher named Billingsley demands their surrender and a standoff ensues. "'I do not want to kill you in front of my wife and children,' father said. 'But by God, I will! Leave here at once!'" He won the first round; but the affair ended badly for the fugitives and also for Brown and his friends. Tensions between Owen and Lyman rose under the pressure of increased fugitive slave traffic after passage of the 1850 law. Owen attacked Lyman physically, for no apparent reason, and Lyman refused to fight back. They remained friends, but at a certain distance. Part of the problem, psychologically, was that Owen felt Lyman had replaced him in his father's affections. In addition, Owen was subconsciously in love with Lyman's wife. Sensing Owen's attraction to her, Lyman decided he and Susan should return to Timbuctoo. The next winter Brown ordered the two men to cut a trail for running fugitives to the old mining camp in the shadow of a mountain called Cloudsplitter by the Indians. There they were frightened by a ferocious mountain lion. The lion eluded them, but Lyman's gun fired accidentally and killed him. Owen, however, believed *he* killed him in his heart.[37]

In Kansas, as Owen remembers it, he was his father's willing accomplice in terror. The elder brothers, John and Jason, backed off, but Owen turned into a fighter like his father. "O, thou hast lately become a true soldier of the Lord, Owen!" Brown exclaims. Of course, he did not mimic his father's religious mumbo-jumbo. No. What John Brown called God, Owen called history. "And if history, like the will of God, ruled us, then whatever moral dimensions it possessed came not from itself or from above, but from our very acts, and that it would show us our true fates, for good or for evil."[38]

At Harpers Ferry the captain put Owen in charge of a small reserve unit intended to guard the farm and then reinforce the invaders from Maryland once the slaves rose up and the time came to retreat to the mountains. That time never came. Owen, with Barclay Coppoc and Frank Merriam, waited and watched from the heights above the Potomac. He was implored to countermand the order to wait for the slaves but refused, saying, "My father does not want me to save him." Coppoc shook his head: "So, Owen Brown, it's over. And you've single-handedly done the whole thing in. Amazing." Owen had done more than that. He had failed to burn the mass of incriminatory papers in the farmhouse, as ordered. This was the ultimate betrayal. Once he had imagined himself "lurching forward into history on the heels of his father." Now there was nothing left. He made his escape, and by his efforts saved the others. Although Banks does not tell us so, Owen Brown was the only one of the five survivors of Harpers Ferry not to enlist in the Union Army. He became, in some sense, a man without a country. The reader is left with the impression that Owen Brown had finally, at Miss Mayo's prompting, chosen to tell his story for the redemption of his soul. John Brown "made the gallows as glorious as the Cross." His soul went marching on. But for Owen Brown, in Russell Banks's astonishing novel, there was no redemption.[39]

• • IN THE year 2000, the 200th anniversary of his birth, the historic John Brown obtained more exposure to the American public than he ever had through the pages of a book. The Public Broadcasting System (PBS) screened a ninety-minute documentary film, *John Brown's Holy War,* in prime time. In the prologue, Brown is portrayed as a radical reformer, "fighting for the American creed" in the spirit of Thomas Jefferson and his maxim "that a little rebellion, now and then, is a good thing, and as necessary in the political world as storms in the physical." Produced and directed by Robert Kenner, the film follows Brown from his twelfth year, when he witnessed the beating of a black boy. It employs the usual format of talking-heads commentary. Russell Banks stands out in this group, made up largely of historians of the Civil War era. The film does not ignore Brown's faults and foibles, but it is openly sympathetic to him and his cause. The hero's "designed act of martyrdom," Banks says, was brilliantly staged. The film concludes with the observation, "The legend of John Brown took on different meanings."[40]

Banks was one of a group of writers, intellectuals, and activists dedicated to reviving the annual pilgrimage to the North Elba grave on John Brown Day, May 9. A young Bowdoin College historian, Noel Ignatiev, who advocated a repudiation of "white" racial identity, organized the first visit in 1999.[41] John Brown seemed still to have a future in American thought and imagination. Occasionally he even broke into the daily news, as in the matter of the alleged martyrdom of Timothy McVeigh, the bomber of the McMurrah Federal Building in Oklahoma City in 1997. Was that not like John Brown? some asked. "Father of American Terrorism" was the alarming title of a feature article in *American Heritage.*[42] Its author, Ken Chowder, also crafted the scenario of *John Brown's Holy War.* The article follows the documentary film. It does *not* maintain the shocking proposition of the title, which only obfuscates understanding of the man. In January 2000 the Library of Virginia mounted an exhibit, "Death or Liberty: Gabriel, Nat Turner, and John Brown." It was unusual in bringing together records and artifacts of three seminal events in the violent history of slavery in Virginia from 1800 to 1859. In Connecticut, meanwhile, the Torrington Historical Society launched a renewed effort to raise money to reproduce the John Brown birthplace, consumed by fire in 1918, at a pretty spot now marked by a small stone memorial.

It seems well to end on a musical note, in this instance the folk-life performance artists known as Magpie, whose compact disc *John Brown: Sword and Spirit* appeared in the spring of the millennial year. The songs are spun off from a one-act play created by Greg Artzner, Terry Leonino, and Richard Henzel dramatizing the visit of Mary Brown to her husband's jail cell on the eve of his execution. Most of the eleven songs were written by Artzner and Leonino, though Woody Guthrie and others are also represented. The songs have a sweet and haunting quality. They are about Captain Brown, his wife and daughter Annie, Douglass and Harriet Tubman and other allies, and several of the raiders. Reggie and Kim Harris's beautiful ballad "Heaven Is Less than Fair" tells of the Underground Railroad. The lead song, "Old John Brown," by Si Kahn, evokes the captain at Harpers Ferry, when

> The clouds of war are low and dark
> Waitin' for someone to light the spark.

It sings of his journey to the gallows, where he kisses the black child, ascends the stairs, waves off remorse, manfully takes the rope as a gift, and hangs in the raging air. The soldiers tremble as they cut him down. They still feel "the spirit of old John Brown."[43]

Coda

BY PURSUING the track of the John Brown legend through
time, one can begin to understand how malleable is a single
finite human life enacted on the grand stage of history. Brown
gained fame in the course of events leading to the Civil War; indeed,
it was his martyrdom at Harpers Ferry that would make that great
conflict truly "irrepressible." And through the chance of a popular
wartime song, his soul went marching on through all the battles, the
sorrows, and the triumphs of five years of strife.

Characteristically among historical actors, fame is an accretion,
something built up over time. With John Brown it came like thunder all at once. He was unknown to history until his fifty-fifth year,
and still virtually unknown until the dramatic action that culminated
in his death on the scaffold. He would come to be defined by his
martyrdom. The manner of his death was infinitely more important
than his life. Largely for this reason, it is impossible to separate the
record of his life—his biography, if you will—from the legend gathered round him. It is as if the historical John Brown has unfolded
layer after layer as successive generations of inquirers, both proponents and opponents of his fame, have imagined him to have been.
His biography is less an existential thing than a work of intelligence
and imagination, ever changing in answer to new questions and purposes.

John Brown did not lack mixture and complexity in his own person, yet in comparison with the great figures of history, he was narrowly self-contained, with little variability or subtlety in the composition. His creed, moral, political, and otherwise, came down to two tenets: the biblical Golden Rule and the "all men are created equal" of the Declaration of Independence. Nothing could be more American than that. Seeking a metaphor to describe his tightly wound personality and his stern purpose, Stephen Benét said Brown was like nothing so much as a stone, dense, compact, adamantine, and like a stone he chafed and burned.

The simple antonyms of the John Brown image—saint and devil, prophet and madman—gradually fell away as scholars, poets, artists gained new perspectives on the figure. It remains malleable, still open to contingency and challenge. The course of his reputation has fluctuated, and while it seems clear that Brown will never again knock at the door of the American pantheon, he still answers to some of the most enduring moral quandaries and dilemmas of our national life, and these resonate through the image.

Notes

I. THE JOHN BROWN EPOCH

1. *Annual Report of the American Anti-Slavery Society* (New York, 1861), 92–93.
2. Ibid., 93; Craig A. Simpson, *A Good Southerner: The Life of Henry A. Wise of Virginia* (Chapel Hill, 1985), chap. 11.
3. Louis Ruchames, ed., *John Brown: The Making of a Revolutionary* (New York, 1969), 129.
4. Frederick Douglass, *Life and Times of Frederick Douglass,* in his *Prose Works: Selections* (New York, 1994), 717–18.
5. Richard Henry Dana Jr., "How We Met John Brown," *Atlantic Monthly* 28 (1871): 1–9.
6. Oswald Garrison Villard, *John Brown, 1800–1859* (Gloucester, Mass., 1965), 248.
7. James Redpath, ed., *Echoes of Harper's Ferry* (New York, 1969), 307.
8. Villard, *John Brown,* 392–93.
9. *Richmond Dispatch,* Oct. 20, 1859; *National Era,* Oct. 27, 1859.
10. *Charleston Mercury,* Oct. 27, 31, Nov. 1, 1859.
11. Ibid., Nov. 21, 28, 1859. Cf. Steven Channing, *Crisis of Fear* (New York, 1970), chap. 1.
12. *New-York Tribune,* Nov. 3, 1859.
13. *Annual Report,* 109–11.
14. George S. Merriam, *The Life and Times of Samuel Bowles* (New York, 1885), 1:252.
15. Quoted in *Chicago Press and Tribune,* Nov. 5, 1859; and Villard, *John Brown,* 501.
16. Quoted in *Boston Daily Advertiser,* Nov. 5, 1859.
17. Redpath, *Echoes of Harper's Ferry,* 262; Villard, *John Brown,* 519n.
18. Redpath, *Echoes of Harper's Ferry,* 55.
19. Ibid., 16–42.

20. *Boston Daily Advertiser,* Nov. 22, 1859; *Chicago Tribune,* Dec. 3, 1859; *Independent,* quoted in *Liberator,* Dec. 2, 1859; *National Era,* Nov. 24, 1859.

21. Thomas Jefferson, *Notes on the State of Virginia,* Query XVIII, in his *Writings,* ed. Merrill D. Peterson (New York, 1984), 289.

22. *New-York Tribune,* Nov. 29, 1859; *Richmond Dispatch,* Nov. 7, 24, 26, 28, 1859; *De Bow's Review,* quoted in Charles F. Heller, *Portrait of an Abolitionist: A Biography of George Luther Stearns* (Westport, Conn., 1996), 107.

23. Nathaniel Cabell to Henry S. Randall, Jan. 6, 1860, in Cabell Papers, Virginia Historical Society, Richmond.

24. Lydia Maria Francis Child, *Lydia Maria Child, Selected Letters, 1817–1888,* ed. Milton Meltzer and Patricia Holland (Amherst, Mass., 1982), 322–25, 329.

25. *National Anti-Slavery Standard,* Dec. 3, 1859; Thomas Russell quoted in *Magazine of Western History* 10 (1889): 19.

26. Villard, *John Brown,* 551, 554; *New-York Tribune,* Dec. 5, 1859.

27. *Chicago Tribune,* Dec. 5, 1859; Col. J. T. L. Preston to Margaret Preston, in *Confederate Veteran* 8 (1900): 47–48. Cf. *Annual Report,* 127–28; and Murat Halstead, "The Tragedy of John Brown," *Independent* 50 (1898): 541–48. For the Booth quotation: David Grimsted, *American Mobbing, 1828–1861* (New York, 1998), 276.

28. *Liberator,* Dec. 9, 1859; Emerson, quoted in Robert D. Richardson Jr., *Emerson: The Mind on Fire* (Berkeley, 1995), 545; Emerson, *Miscellanies: Works* (Boston, 1891), 7:28, 209.

29. Redpath, *Echoes of Harper's Ferry,* 204, 209, 354.

30. *Letters of Henry Wadsworth Longfellow,* ed. Andrew Hilen, 6 vols. (Cambridge, Mass., 1966–82), 4:3; Howells and Proctor in Redpath, *Echoes of Harper's Ferry,* 316, 124.

31. *Oxford Anthology of American Literature* (New York, 1938), 2:856–58.

32. John Greenleaf Whittier, *The Complete Poetical Works of John Greenleaf Whittier* (Boston, 1892), 201. Cf. Roland H. Woodwill, *John Greenleaf Whittier: A Biography* (Haverhill, Mass., 1955), 289.

33. *Liberator,* Oct. 28, 1859; Redpath, *Echoes of Harper's Ferry,* 305–15; Laurence J. Friedman, "Violent Means," *Psychohistory Review* 9 (1980): 23–59.

34. James D. Breeden, "Rehearsal for Secession? The Return of Southern Medical Students from Philadelphia in 1859," in *His Soul Goes Marching On,* ed. Paul Finkelman (Charlottesville, 1995). Cf. Hunter McGuire, "Annual Report of Sons of Confederate Veterans," *Confederate Veteran* 7 (1899), and L. A. Wailes, "The First Secessionists," *Confederate Veteran* 30 (1922).

35. Wendell Phillips, *Speeches, Lectures, and Letters* (Boston, 1884), 290–91; Leonard Twynham, "A Martyr for John Brown," *Opportunity* 16 (1938): 205; "The Funeral of John Brown," *New England Magazine* 30 (1904): 229–43.

36. For Everett, *New-York Tribune*, Jan. 16, 1860; U.S. Congress, Senate, Select Committee on the Harper's Ferry Invasion, *Invasion at Harper's Ferry* (New York, 1969), 68, 88, 242, 245, and passim.

37. Ibid., 245.

38. Ibid., 1–25.

39. Abraham Lincoln, *The Collected Works of Abraham Lincoln*, ed. Roy P. Basler (New Brunswick, N.J., 1952), 3:496, 5:278.

40. Robert Hendrickson, *Sumter: The First Day in the Civil War* (Washington, 1990), 22–23; Betty L. Mitchell, *Edmund Ruffin: A Biography* (Bloomington, Ind., 1981), 140; *Confederate Veteran* 25 (1917): 108.

2. FACES AND PLACES OF THE HERO

1. Ralph Waldo Emerson, *Works: Journals and Miscellaneous Notebooks*, ed. Ronald A. Bosco and Glen Jackson (Cambridge, Mass., 1982), 15:468.

2. First printed in *Independent*, Aug. 8, 1861, then reprinted in *Independent* 69 (1910): 115; J. H. Jenkin, "The Story of the Song, 'John Brown's Body,'" *Western Pennsylvania History Magazine* 34 (1920): 212–13, copied from *The Collector*, June 1910; George Kimball, "Origin of the John Brown Song," *New England Magazine* 1 (1885): 271–72; Boyd B. Stutler, *Glory, Glory Hallelujah!* (Cincinnati, 1960).

3. *Independent* 69 (1910): 116.

4. Laura E. Richardson and Maude Howe Elliott, eds., *Julia Ward Howe, 1819–1910* (Boston, 1915), 1:177, 187–88.

5. C. B. Galbreath, "Edwin Coppoc" and "Barclay Coppoc," *Ohio Archeological and Historical Society Publications* 30 (1921): 397–445, 459–81; Thomas Tinkler, "The Rendition of Barclay Coppoc," *Iowa Journal of History and Politics* 10 (1912): 503–66; J. K. Hudson, "The John Brown League," in Oswald Garrison Villard Papers, Columbia University; E. C. Lampson, "Black Passions: A Historical Narrative of the Sons of Liberty, and of the Western Reserve," typescript, 1930, Library of Congress.

6. James Monroe, *Oberlin Thursday Lectures: Addresses and Essays* (Oberlin, 1897); William Cheek and Aimee Lee Cheek, *John Mercer Langston and the Fight for Black Freedom, 1829–65* (Urbana, 1989).

7. Franklin B. Sanborn, *Life and Letters of John Brown: Liberator of Kansas, and Martyr of Virginia* (Boston, 1885), 630–31.

8. Quoted in Martin B. Pasternak, *Rise and Fly to Arms: The Life of Henry Highland Garnet* (New York, 1995), 95; Henry G. Pearson, *Life of John Andrew* (Boston, 1904), 1:100, 2:51n.

9. Oswald Garrison Villard, *John Brown: A Biography Fifty Years After* (Boston, 1910), 550; Caroline B. Sherman, "A Neglected Boy in the Civil War," *New England*

Quarterly 5 (1932): 315; G. A. Townsend, "Letter to Chicago Tribune" (1869), copy in Virginia Historical Society, Richmond.

10. George Templeton Strong, *The Diary of George Templeton Strong*, ed. Allan Nevins and M. H. Thorn (New York, 1952), 544.

11. Francis H. Pierpont to an unnamed correspondent, n.d., typescript copy in Virginia Historical Society; *New-York Tribune*, Oct. 5, 1884; Craig M. Simpson, *A Good Southerner: The Life of Henry A. Wise of Virginia* (Chapel Hill, 1985), 292.

12. *Osawatomie Brown* (New York, 1859); "An Old Play on John Brown," *Kansas Historical Quarterly* 6 (1937): 34–59.

13. James Redpath, *The Roving Editor; or Talks with Slaves*, ed. John R. McKinigan (University Park, Pa., 1996), 3–5.

14. James Redpath, *The Public Life of Capt. John Brown, with an Auto-Biography of His Childhood and Youth* (Boston, 1860), 38–39, 54–55.

15. Ibid., 58. See also *Boston Daily Advertiser*, Nov. 9, 1859.

16. Redpath, *Public Life*, 103–4, 187, 115, 149.

17. Charles E. Heller, *Portrait of an Abolitionist: A Biography of George Luther Stearns* (Westport, Conn., 1996), 142; Robert H. Semmes, "Lydia Maria Child . . . , Brackett's Bust of John Brown," *American Literature* 40 (1968), 539–42; Walter Muir Whitehill, "John Brown of Osawatomie in Boston, 1857," *Proceedings of Massachusetts Historical Society* 69 (1950): 270, 272.

18. Heller, *Portrait of an Abolitionist*, 147.

19. "John Brown and the Colored Child," in *The Freedmen's Book*, ed. Lydia Maria Child (Boston, 1865), 241–42.

20. Redpath, *Public Life*, 397.

21. James C. Malin, "The Legend of John Brown in Pictures: Kissing the Negro Baby," *Kansas Historical Quarterly* 8 (1939): 339–46. See also Cecil D. Eby, Jr., "Whittier's 'Brown of Osawatomie,'" *New England Quarterly* 33 (1960): 452–61.

22. *New-York Tribune*, Aug. 27, 1882, reprinting from *Louisville Commercial; Memphis Sunday Times*, Aug. 9, 1885, clipping, Boyd B. Stutler Collection, West Virginia Historical Society; *Springfield Republican*, 1899, clipping, Clarence S. Gee Collection, Hudson (Ohio) Library and Historical Society.

23. *Southern Historical Society Papers* 13 (1885): 339–44; Bernard Weisberger, *Reporters for the Union* (Boston, 1953), 71–72; Boyd B. Stutler, "Olcott Leaflet," John Brown Collection, Manuscript Division, Library of Congress.

24. George W. Putnam, "The Sacrifice," *Douglass' Monthly*, Nov. 3, 1860.

25. Reprint from *Lake Placid News*, May 18, 1928, John Brown Collection, Oberlin College Library.

26. George Washington Williams, *History of the Negro Race in America* (New York, 1882), 2:214–22.

27. *New York Times*, Dec. 27, 1878.

28. Frederick Douglass, *Life and Times of Frederick Douglass*, in his *Prose Works: Selections* (New York, 1994), chap. 17.

29. *New York Times*, Aug. 22, 24; Sept. 5; Oct. 27, 31; Nov. 17, 1882; *Chicago Tribune*, Aug. 22, 25, 27, 1882.

30. J. W. Beeman, "Reminiscence," March 1884, in John Brown Collection, Kansas State Historical Society, Topeka.

31. *New-York Tribune*, Apr. 1, 1894.

32. Kate Field, *Correspondence: Selections*, ed. Carolyn J. Mass (Carbondale, Ill., 1996), 220n.

33. Henry Bowditch, quoted in Hermann von Holst, *John Brown* (Boston, 1889), Appendix.

34. See Thomas Featherstonhaugh, "The Final Burial of the Followers of John Brown," *New England Magazine* 24 (1901): 128–34; *New York World*, Sept. 21, 1895.

35. *New England Magazine* 10 (1894): 272–81.

36. William R. Lingo, *The Pennsylvania Career of John Brown* (Carney, Pa., 1926); Ernest C. Miller, *John Brown: Pennsylvania Citizen* (Warren, Pa., 1952); Boyd Stutler, "John Brown, Pennsylvania Farmer," *Service Magazine* (1930), in Stutler Collection.

37. John Keith, "John Brown as a Poet," *Magazine of Western History* 10 (1889): 19.

38. *New-York Tribune*, suppl., May 6, 1899.

39. Sanborn, *Life and Letters*, 88.

40. Edmund Brown, in *Midwestern Congregationalist* (1892), also in *John Brown: The Making of a Revolutionary*, ed. Louis Ruchames (New York, 1959), 187–89; and see Will M. Clemons, "John Brown, the American Reformer," *Peterson's Magazine*, n.s. 8 (1898), 27.

41. Ruchames, *John Brown*, 189–90.

42. Louis Filler, "John Brown in Ohio: An Interview . . . ," *Ohio Archaeological Quarterly* 58 (1949): 213–18.

43. Daniel B. Hodley, "Reminiscences of John Brown," *McClure's Magazine* 10 (1898): 278–88. See also Mary Land, "John Brown's Ohio Environment," *Ohio Archaeological Quarterly* 57 (1948): 24–47.

44. Irving B. Richmond, *John Brown among the Quakers* (Des Moines, 1894), 23.

45. Benjamin F. Gue, *History of Iowa* (New York, 1903), 1:chap. 29; J. E. Todd, "John Brown's Last Visit," *Annals of Iowa* 3 (1898): 458–61; Charles E. Payne, *Joseph Bushnell Grinnell* (Iowa City, 1938), 111–12.

46. Gue, *History of Iowa,* 1:380.

47. Benjamin F. Gue, "John Brown's Betrayer," *New-York Tribune,* Feb. 1, 1897.

3. THE KANSAS IMBROGLIO

1. James C. Malin, *John Brown and the Legend of Fifty-six,* Memoirs of the American Philosophical Society, vol. 17 (Philadelphia, 1942), 355; *New-York Tribune,* Sept. 1, 1877.

2. Malin, *John Brown,* 437.

3. William A. Phillips, "Three Interviews with Old John Brown," *Atlantic Monthly* 28 (1879): 738–44.

4. William A. Phillips, "Lights and Shadows of Kansas History," *Magazine of Western History* 12 (1890): 6–12.

5. James Townsley, "The Pottawatomie Tragedy," in *John Brown: The Making of a Revolutionary,* ed. Louis Ruchames, 205–11 (New York, 1859).

6. Ibid., 46, 202.

7. Charles Robinson, *The Kansas Conflict* (New York, 1892), 329, 393–94, 487.

8. George Washington Brown, *The Truth at Last: History Corrected. Reminiscences of Old John Brown* (Rockford, Ill., 1880).

9. Quoted in Malin, *John Brown,* 405.

10. David N. Utter, "John Brown of Osawatomie," *North American Review* 137 (1883): 435–46; John Ingalls, "John Brown's Place in History," ibid. 138 (1884): 138–50; "Utter Scrapbook," 1880–84, in Boyd B. Stutler Collection, West Virginia Historical Society, Charleston.

11. *Boston Daily Advertiser,* Sept. 15, 1879.

12. Eli Thayer, *A History of the Kansas Crusade, Its Friends and Foes (New York, 1889);* John G. Nicolay and John Hay, *Abraham Lincoln: A History* (New York, 1890).

13. Franklin B. Sanborn, ed., *The Life and Letters of John Brown: Liberator of Kansas, and Martyr of Virginia* (Boston, 1885), 185.

14. Ibid., 128.

15. Ibid., 247.

16. Wendell P. Garrison, "The Prelude to Harper's Ferry," *Andover Review* 14 (1890): 778–87.

17. Sanborn, *Life and Letters,* 248, 263.

18. Ibid., 490n.

19. F. B. Sanborn, *Recollections of Seventy Years,* 2 vols. (Boston, 1909), 1:91–93; Robinson, *Kansas Conflict,* appendix, 482–87.

20. Sanborn, *Life and Letters,* 446.

21. Sanborn, *Recollections,* 1:229–43; "A Concord Note-Book," *Critic* 47 (1895): 349–56; Octavius Brooks Frothingham, *Gerrit Smith: A Biography* (New York, 1878),

chap. 6; J. Wade Carruthers, *Octavius Brooks Frothingham, Gentle Radical* (University, Ala., 1977), 151–52.

22. John Brown Clippings, 1:153, Kansas State Historical Society, Topeka; Lydia Maria Child to Mrs. Archibald, Jan. 8, 1860, Manuscripts Collection, New York Public Library.

23. Leverett W. Spring, "Catching Old John Brown," *Overland Monthly*, 2d ser., 1 (1883): 564–68; J. W. Winkley, *John Brown the Hero* (Boston, 1905), 46, 81.

24. *St. Louis Daily Globe-Democrat*, Apr. 8, 1888, in John Brown Clippings, vol. 7, Kansas State Historical Society; Andrew Hunter, "John Brown's Raid," *Publications of the Southern Historical Association* 1, no. 3 (1897): 165–95 (first published in a Virginia newspaper in 1887).

25. Albion Tourgee, *Hot Plowshares* (New York, 1882), 608–9.

26. John Brown Clippings, 10:131; and Mrs. Stearns to Mrs. Brown, Dec. 2, 1860, in George and Mary Stearns Collection, both in Kansas State Historical Society.

27. Franklin G. Adams to Mrs. Stearns, Aug. 23, 1889, in Stearns Collection.

28. The story of the Brackett bust may be found in Sanborn, *Life and Letters*, 515–16.

29. J. B. Heywood statement, May 25, 1886, in Stearns Collection.

30. Richard J. Hinton, *John Brown and His Men* (New York, 1894), 202–5.

31. Hermann von Holst, *John Brown* (Boston, 1889), 92, 107, 111.

32. George W. Curtis, *Orations and Addresses* (New York, 1893).

33. William Herbert Carruth, "John Brown," *New England Magazine* 7 (1892): 173.

34. Eugene Ware, "John Brown," in his *Rhymes of Ironquill* (Topeka, 1889).

35. William Elsey Connelly, *John Brown* (Topeka, 1900), 171–72, 205.

36. *Nation* 91 (1910): 207.

37. Robert G. Athearn, *In Search of Caanan: Black Migration to Kansas, 1879–80* (Lawrence, Kans., 1978), 32.

38. John Brown Clippings, 13:234, in Kansas State Historical Society.

39. *New-York Tribune*, July 29 and Aug. 30, 1906.

4. THE GREAT BIOGRAPHY

1. *Letters of Charles Eliot Norton, with Biographical Comment by His Daughter . . .* (Boston, 1913), 1:197–201.

2. Thomas Carlyle, *Heroes, Hero-Worship and the Heroic in History* (Boston, 1902), 132–33.

3. Hermann E. von Holst, *Constitutional and Political History of the United States*, vol. 6 (New York, 1892); Marcus J. Wright, "The Trial and Execution of John Brown," *Papers of the American Historical Association* 4 (1890): 439–54; James Schouler, *History of the United States of America, under the Constitution* (New York, 1880), 5:437–47.

4. John W. Burgess, *The Civil War and the Constitution, 1859–1865* (New York, 1901), 1:36–38; French Ensor Chadwick, *Causes of the Civil War, 1859–1861* (New York, 1906), 350–51; Albert Bushnell Hart to Oswald Garrison Villard, Dec. 1, 1907, in Brown-Villard Papers, Columbia University.

5. Woodrow Wilson, *A History of the American People*, 5 vols. (New York, 1902), 4:184–87; R. G. Horton, *Youth's History of the Great Civil War in the United States* (New York, 1867), 61; John A. Wyeth, *With Sabre and Scalpel: The Autobiography of a Soldier and Surgeon* (New York, 1914), 94, 124.

6. James Ford Rhodes, *History of the United States from the Compromise of 1850* (New York, 1910), 2:165, 397, 399.

7. Edward Channing, *A History of the United States* (New York, 1925), 6:219–25.

8. Rhodes, *History*, 2:411.

9. Elbert Hubbard, *Time and Chance, A Romance and a History* (East Aurora, N.Y., 1899), 249, 434.

10. Villard to Sanborn, Mar. 9, 1909, in Brown-Villard Papers.

11. Oswald Garrison Villard, *John Brown, 1800–1859: A Biography Fifty Years After* (Gloucester, Mass., 1965), vii.

12. Sanborn to Villard, Oct. 8, 1910, in Brown-Villard Papers; Stephen B. Oates, *To Purge This Land with Blood: A Biography of John Brown* (Amherst, Mass., 1984), 364n; David Lines Jacobus, "Peter Brown of Windsor, Connecticut," *American Genealogist* 33 (1957): 214–22; Gerald W. McFarland, *A Scattered People: An American Family Moves West* (New York, 1985), 13.

13. *National Anti-Slavery Standard*, Dec. 24, 1859; Thomas Hughes, *The Manliness of Christ* (New York, 1880).

14. In *Nation* 98 (1914): 157.

15. Villard, *John Brown*, 16–18.

16. Ibid., 23.

17. Villard to Sanborn, Oct. 8, 1909, and William Tatham to Wise, Nov. 8, 1859, in Brown-Villard Papers.

18. Villard, *John Brown*, 48, 36.

19. Ibid., 54–55, 79.

20. Ibid., 77–78.

21. Katherine Mayo and Villard letters, Aug. 3 and 8, 1908, and July 16, 1908, in Brown-Villard Papers.

22. Villard to Mayo, April 23, June 6, 1908, Brown-Villard Papers; Villard, *John Brown*, 184.

23. Villard, *John Brown*, 230, 262.

24. Ibid., 266.

25. Ibid., 285, 332, 224, 336.

26. Ibid., 408, 416–20.

27. Ibid., 424–25.

28. Ibid., 455, 450.

29. Ibid., 415, 509–10.

30. Ibid., 514, 580.

31. Ibid., 528.

32. "Dr. S. G. Howe on John Brown's Raid," *Nation* 89 (1909): 302–3; Villard to Hart, May 5, 1910, and Sanborn–Villard exchange, Oct. 26 and 29, 1909, in Brown-Villard Papers; Villard, *John Brown,* 530–33.

33. Howe–Villard exchange, Oct. 27, Nov. 23, 1910, in Brown-Villard Papers; Villard, *John Brown,* 533.

34. Villard, *John Brown,* 586–89.

35. Sanborn to Villard, Oct. 8, 1910; W. C. Ford to Villard, Dec. 27, 1910, and Feb. 2, 1911; Samuel Bowles to Villard, Feb. 23, 1911, all in Brown-Villard Papers.

36. *North American Review* 193 (1910): 26–34, 35–41.

37. *Atlantic Monthly* 106 (1910): 662–68.

38. Villard to Higginson, Oct. 27, 1909, in Brown-Villard Papers; *Horizon* 5 (1909).

39. Address, in *Pamphlets . . . of W. E. B. Du Bois,* ed. Herbert Aptheker (White Plains, N.Y., 1981), 63–65.

40. W. E. B. Du Bois, *John Brown* (1909), ed. David Smith (London, 1997), xix, 33, 175, 195.

41. Irving B. Richman to Villard, Sept. 12, 1911, and William R. Thayer to Villard, Aug. 31, 1910, in Brown-Villard Papers; Carter G. Woodson, ed., *The Mind of the Negro as Reflected in Letters Written during the Crisis, 1800–1860* (Washington, D.C., 1926), 506; *Tyler's Quarterly* 1, (1920): 223; *Virginia Magazine of History* 25 (1917): 334.

42. Ely Moore, Jr., "The Naming of Osawatomie," *Kansas Historical Collections* 12 (1911): 338–47.

43. *Chicago Tribune,* Aug. 29 and Sept. 1, 1910; *New York Times,* Aug. 31 and Sept. 1, 1910.

44. Theodore Roosevelt, *Letters,* ed. Elting Morison (Cambridge, Mass., 1951), 7:108n; Roosevelt to Lyman Draper, ibid., 193–94, 198.

45. See Dan W. Wilson, *Governor Charles Robinson of Kansas* (Lawrence, Kans., 1975), chaps. 5 and 6.

46. Hill Peebles Wilson, *John Brown, Soldier of Fortune: A Critique* (Lawrence, Kans., 1913), 404, 344.

47. Oswald Garrison Villard, "Historical Verity," *Collections of the Kansas State Historical Society* 12 (1913–14): 423–29.

5 . KALEIDOSCOPE

1. Kenneth Durant, "Lincoln and Brown," *Nation* 109 (1919): 292–93.

2. Lord Charnwood, *Abraham Lincoln* (New York, 1917), 150–55.

3. Stephen Graham, *The Soul of John Brown* (New York, 1920), 328–31.

4. Parry Stroud, *Stephen Vincent Benét* (New York, 1962), 46; *Notes and Queries* 53 (1929): 186–89; Stephen Vincent Benét, *John Brown's Body* (Boston, 1928), 31, 55–56.

5. Benét, *John Brown's Body*, 344, 373–74, 376.

6. *Playbill*, New Century Theatre, 1953, in Special Collections, Alderman Library, University of Virginia; *New York Times*, Feb. 16 and 22, 1953; Simon Callow, *Charles Laughton: A Difficult Actor* (New York, 1997), 216–20.

7. See John Drinkwater, *American Vignettes, 1860–1865* (Boston, 1931).

8. *New Statesman and Nation* 5 (1933): 569–70.

9. Michael Blankfort and Michael Gold, *Battle Hymn* (New York, 1936), 43, 70–71.

10. Kirke Mechem, *John Brown: A Play in Three Acts* (Manhattan, Kans., 1939).

11. Thomas Dixon, *The Torch: A Story of the Paranoiac Who Caused a Great War, Written Directly for the Screen* (n.p., n.d. [1927]), 10, 107, 117.

12. Thomas Dixon, *The Man in Gray: A Romance of North and South* (New York, 1921), 17.

13. Oswald Garrison Villard, "History and the Movies," *Saturday Review of Literature* 23 (1940): 9.

14. See the epilogue in the manuscript of Velma West Sykes, "Widowed by the Gallows: A Biography of Mrs. John Brown," in John Brown Papers, Manuscript Division, Library of Congress.

15. Allen Tate, "On the Martyr of Harper's Ferry," *Sewanee Review* 38 (1930): 29; Charles M. Sheldon, "God's Angry Man," *Independent* 69 (1910): 113; Coates Kinney, "John Brown," *Ohio Archaeological and Historical Society Publications* 30 (1921): 183; *The Poetry of Vachel Lindsay*, ed. Dennis Camp (Peoria, 1984), 319–22; "The Ballad of John Brown," *Daily Worker*, Dec. 26, 1939; Countee Cullen, "A Negro Mother's Lullaby," *Opportunity*, Jan. 1942, 7.

16. Edwin Arlington Robinson, "John Brown," in his *Collected Poems* (New York, 1930), 485–90.

17. Muriel Rukeyser, "The Soul and Body of John Brown," *Poetry* 56 (1940): 115–20; Untermeyer is quoted in Louise Kertesz, *The Poetic Vision of Muriel Rukeyser* (Baton Rouge, 1980), 168–71.

18. Robert Penn Warren, *Robert Penn Warren Talking: Interviews, 1950–1978*, ed. Floyd C. Watkins and John T. Hiers (New York, 1980), 180; James H. Jackson, *The Achievement of Robert Penn Warren* (Baton Rouge, 1981), 150; Charles Bohner, *Robert Penn Warren* (Boston, 1981), 20.

19. Robert Penn Warren, *John Brown: The Making of a Martyr* (Nashville, 1929), 226–27.

20. Ibid., 125, 206, 445, 414, 210; Warren, *Warren Talking*, 181.

21. Warren, *Making of a Martyr*, 62, 331–32, 261–62; Warren, *Warren Talking*, 175–76.

22. David Karsner, *John Brown, Terrible "Saint"* (New York, 1934), 186.

23. Leonard Ehrlich, *God's Angry Man* (New York, 1932), 67, 76, 179, 279.

24. Gamaliel Bradford, *Journal of Gamaliel Bradford, 1883–1932*, ed. Van Wyck Brooks (Boston, 1933), 236, 265.

25. Gamaliel Bradford, *Damaged Souls* (Boston, 1923), 159–60, 171, 178, 180, 185.

26. Carl Sandburg, *Abraham Lincoln: The Prairie Years* (New York, 1926), 2:194.

27. John Cournos, *A Modern Plutarch* (Indianapolis, 1928), 207–34; Dixon Wecter, *Hero in America: A Chronicle of Hero Worship* (New York, 1941), 250.

28. Ernest Kaiser in *Black Titan: W. E. B. Du Bois: An Anthology*, ed. John Henrik Clarke et al. (Boston, 1970), 120; J. G. Randall, *The Civil War and Reconstruction* (Boston, 1937), 139, 173; Allan Nevins, *Ordeal of the Union, 2 vols.* (New York, 1947), 2:473–474.

29. James C. Malin, *John Brown and the Legend of Fifty-six*, Memoirs of the American Philosophical Society, vol. 17 (Philadelphia, 1942), viii, 3, 19, 23, passim.

30. Ibid., 243, 245, 701.

31. Ibid., 317–18 (italics in original).

32. Ibid., 425, 754–55, 695–96.

33. Ibid., 695–96.

34. Ralph V. Harlow, in *Journal of Southern History* 9 (1943): 418–19.

35. *Dictionary of American Biography* (New York, 1930), 2:131–34; Ray A. Billington, *Westward Expansion: A History of the American Frontier*, rev. ed. (New York, 1960), 604; C. Vann Woodward, "John Brown's Private War," in *America in Crisis: Fourteen Crucial Episodes in American History*, ed. Daniel Aaron (New York, 1952), 109–32. For a review of John Brown in school textbooks, see James W. Loewens, *Lies My Teachers Told Me* (New York, 1995), 165–93.

36. Samuel M. Le Page, "Memoirs of John Brown of Osawatomie," *Current History* 28 (1928): 427–30.

37. Boyd Stutler to Clarence Gee, June 14, 1958, in Stutler–Gee Correspondence, Hudson Library and Historical Society.

38. Stutler to Gee, Dec. 8, 1957, and Nov. 24, 1953, ibid.

39. Gee to Stutler, March 27, 1953, ibid.

40. *New York Times*, May 22, 1932; Apr. 28, 1935; May 9, 10, 1935.

41. The letter, undated, is in Powell Family Papers, Virginia Historical Society, Richmond.

42. William C. Hueston and J. Finley Wilson, *The John Brown Reader* (Washington, D.C., 1949).

43. Patricia Junker, ed., *John Steuart Curry: Inventing the Middle West* (New York, 1998), 217 and passim; M. Sue Kendall, *Rethinking Regionalism: John Steuart Curry and the Kansas Mural Controversy* (Washington, D.C., 1986); *New York Times*, Nov. 27, 1937.

44. Quoted in *Newsweek*, July 7, 1941, 58; and *Topeka Journal*, Jan. 28, 1941.

45. *New York Times*, Aug. 31, 1946.

46. Bertram D. Wolfe, *Diego Rivera: Portrait of America* (New York, 1937), 123 and passim; Karal Ann Marling, *Wall-to-Wall America: Post Office Murals in the Great Depression* (Minneapolis, 1982), 192.

47. Robert Hayden, "John Brown," in his *Collected Poems* (New York, 1985), 149–53. For Lawrence, see in general Ellen Harkins Wheat, *Jacob Lawrence: The Frederick Douglass and Harriet Tubman Series of 1938–40* (Seattle, 1991); *Newsweek,* Dec. 24, 1945; *Art Digest* 20 (1945): 17.

48. Richard J. Powell, "Re-creating American History," in *I Tell My Heart: The Art of Horace Pippin,* ed. Judith E. Stein, 70–80 (Philadelphia, 1993).

49. Adelyn D. Breeskin, *William H. Johnson, 1901–1970* (Washington, D.C., 1971), 18, 114.

50. *Daily Worker,* May 29, 1941.

51. Marcy Heidish, *A Woman Called Moses* (Boston, 1976), 209.

52. William Branch's *In Splendid Error* is included in *Black Theater: A Twentieth Century Collection of the Work of Its Best Playwrights,* ed. Lindsay Patterson, 93–133 (New York, 1971), 119, 120, 131–33.

6. JOHN BROWN REDIVIVUS

1. *Congressional Record,* 85th Cong., 2d sess., 7714; 86th Cong., 1st sess., 18795–97; *New York Times,* Oct. 4 and Nov. 8, 1959; *Evening Star* (Washington, D.C.), Sept. 7, 1959.

2. *Chicago Defender,* Apr. 4, Oct. 17, Oct. 24, 1959; Langston Hughes, *The Complete Langston Hughes,* ed. Arnold Rampersand (New York, 1988), 2:638; Langston Hughes, *One-Way Ticket* (New York, 1949), 89.

3. *Chicago Defender,* Nov. 7, 1959; W. E. B. Du Bois, "The Crucifixion of John Brown," *New Times* (Moscow, 1959), in *Writings by W. E. B. Du Bois in Periodicals Edited by Others,* ed. Herbert Aptheker, 4 vols. (Millwood, N.J., 1982), 4:306.

4. Herbert Aptheker, *John Brown* (New York, 1960).

5. See Ernest Kaiser, "J. C. Furnas, Mrs. Stowe, and American Racism," *Freedomways* 1 (1961): 136–45.

6. J. C. Furnas, *The Road to Harpers Ferry* (New York, 1959), 49, 328, 353.

7. J. A. Rogers, "Civil War Centennial: Myth and Reality," *Freedomways* 3 (1963): 7–63.

8. Bruce Catton, *The Coming Fury* (New York, 1961), 19.

9. *New York Times,* Dec. 6, 7, Sept. 3, Nov. 11, 1962; Julia Davis, *The Anvil: The Trial of John Brown* (New York, 1963), 13–14.

10. Truman Nelson, *The Truman Nelson Reader,* ed. William J. Schafer (Amherst, Mass., 1989), 169.

11. Truman Nelson, "John Brown Revisited," *Nation* 185 (1957): 86–88.

12. Truman Nelson, *The Surveyor* (Garden City, N.Y., 1960), 202, 270, 281, 359, 342.

13. Ibid., 464, 471, 478, 498, 501.

14. Nelson, *Nelson Reader*, xx; Truman Nelson, *The Right of Revolution* (Boston, 1968), 5.

15. Albert Fried, *John Brown's Journey: Notes and Reflections on His America and Mine* (Garden City, N.Y. 1978), 4, 276.

16. Benjamin Quarles, *Allies for Freedom: Blacks and John Brown* (New York, 1974), 2.

17. Merrill D. Peterson, *Lincoln in American Memory* (New York, 1994), 357; Lerone Bennett, *The Negro Mood and Other Essays* (Chicago, 1964), 98, 100–104.

18. Malcolm X quoted in *John Brown*, ed. Richard Warch and Jonathan Fanton (Englewood Cliffs, N.J., 1973), 178; *Los Angeles Sentinel*, July 8, 1999.

19. Robert Penn Warren, *Who Speaks for the Negro?* (New York, 1965), 313–22.

20. Lacy Baldwin Smith, *Fools, Martyrs, and Traitors: The Story of Martyrdom in the Western World* (New York, 1997), 249.

21. Stephen B. Oates, *To Purge This Land with Blood: A Biography of John Brown*, 2d ed. (Amherst, Mass., 1984), ix, 390, 221, 224, 334, 397, 410–12.

22. Stephen B. Oates, "John Brown and His Judges: A Critique of the Historical Literature," in *Beyond the Civil War Synthesis: Political Essays on the Civil War Era*, ed. Robert P. Sieringa (Westport, Conn., 1975), 57–72.

23. Truman Nelson, "'You Have Not Studied Them Right,'" *Nation* 212 (1971): 405–7, 546.

24. Jules Abels, *Man on Fire: John Brown and the Cause of Liberty* (New York, 1971), xvii, 3, 7, 76–77, 166, 249–54; Oates, *To Purge This Land*, 209.

25. Laurence Sterne, *The Life and Opinions of Tristram Shandy* (London, 1903), 1:38.

26. Richard O. Boyer, *The Legend of John Brown: A Biography and a History* (New York, 1973), 139–45, 212–17, 263, 458–59, xxiii.

27. Moncure Conway, "Washington and Frederick the Great," *Century* 41 (1891): 945–48.

28. Barrie Stavis, *Harper's Ferry: A Play about John Brown* (New York, 1967), 44; see also Stavis, *John Brown: The Sword and the Word* (New York, 1970).

29. Michael S. Harper, *Images of Kin: New and Selected Poems* (Urbana, 1977), 83.

30. George McDonald Fraser, *Flashman and the Angel of the Lord* (London, 1994), 95, 207, 208, 363.

31. Bruce Olds, *Raising Holy Hell* (New York, 1995), 160.

32. *Washington Post*, Dec. 19, 1996; *New York Times*, Dec. 20, 1996; *A Durable Memento: Portraits by Augustus Washington, African American Daguerreotypist* (Washington, D.C.: Smithsonian National Portrait Gallery, 1996).

33. Robert Delaney, *John Brown's Song* (Boston, 1932).

34. Kirke Mechem, *John Brown: Opera in Three Acts* (New York, n.d.), e; *Kansas City Star,* Dec. 3, 1994.

35. Boyd Stutler to Clarence Gee, Feb. 27, 1949, in Stutler–Gee Correspondence, Hudson Library and Historical Society; "Erick Hawkins Addresses a New Dance Audience," *Dance,* June 1967, 40–42.

36. Russell Banks, *Cloudsplitter* (New York, 1998), 104, 202, 67–68, 73, 421.

37. Ibid., 145, 144, 228.

38. Ibid., 597, 608.

39. Ibid., 744, 688.

40. *John Brown's Holy War* (PBS Home Video, 2000).

41. *Boston Globe,* Feb. 21, 1999.

42. Ken Chowder, "Father of American Terrorism," *American Heritage* 33 (2000): 81–91.

43. Magpie, *John Brown: Sword of the Spirit* (Sliced Bread, 2000).

Index

Italicized page numbers refer to illustrations

Also by Merrill D. Peterson

The Jefferson Image in the American Mind (1960)
Thomas Jefferson and the New Nation: A Biography (1970)
James Madison: A Biography in His Own Words (1974)
Adams and Jefferson: A Revolutionary Dialogue (1976)
Olive Branch and Sword: The Compromise of 1833 (1982)
The Great Triumvirate: Webster, Clay, and Calhoun (1987)
Lincoln in American Memory (1994)
Coming of Age with the "New Republic," 1938–1950 (1999)

Edited by Merrill D. Peterson

Major Crises in American History (1962), with Leonard Levy
*Democracy, Liberty, and Property: State Constitutional Convention
    Debates of the 1820s* (1966)
Thomas Jefferson: A Profile (1966)
The Portable Thomas Jefferson (1975)
Thomas Jefferson: Writings (1984)
Thomas Jefferson: A Reference Biography (1986)
*The Virginia Statute for Religious Freedom: Its Evolution and Conse-
    quences in American History* (1988), with Robert Vaughan
Visitors to Monticello (1989)
The Political Writings of Thomas Jefferson (1993)